DOPE AS DOPAMINE

THE ONLY BOOK YOU NEED TO FLIP YOUR LIFE AROUND.

SRIJITA CHAKRABORTY

A special thanks to *Dr. Rajarshi Neogi* and *Dr. Debanjali Basu.* For proving doctors are truly next to gods. For making me believe in the power of empathy, conversations, medicine & the most important of all— *me.*

Contents

Foreword

A LETTER TO MY 8-YEAR-OLD SELF

Hey, little one,

I wish I could shield you from what's coming, but I can't. Life is about to get tougher, tougher than you ever imagined. Some days, it will feel impossible. Depression will walk beside you like an old friend, whispering that this is all there is.

But listen to me: It gets better.

Not in a neat, fairy-tale way. Not all at once. But slowly, in small, stubborn victories. You'll learn to rewrite your own story. You'll find joy in places you never expected. You'll create a life you want to live.

And this book? This is how I did it. It's the bible I wish I had back then, the one I wrote for myself, and now, for you. You are going to be okay. You're going to be more than okay.

You will be happy. Really happy.

Now go live.

With love,

The Woman You Aspire To Become

Acknowledgements

For Himalay & Baba, this book is a thank- you note to you both. For making me love life again and letting the universe do its magic.

Prologue

To Mummum,

And for anyone who's ever felt stuck, confused, or like they don't belong.

Hey you,

Yeah, you, the one reading this in the middle of a messy, complicated, unpredictable life. The one who maybe feels a little lost, a little behind, a little like you should have figured things out by now.

Let me tell you something no one ever told me when I needed to hear it most:

You're not broken. You're not behind. You're not failing at life.

You're just in the middle of a story you haven't finished writing yet.

And if everything feels heavy right now, if the world seems too fast, too loud, too much, pause. Take a deep breath. Let's start over.

Because this? This is the moment where everything can change.

This book isn't here to tell you how to "fix" yourself. You don't need fixing.

It's here to remind you who you really are beneath all the noise, all the expectations, all the rules you never signed up for.

I want you to imagine something.

Picture yourself years from now. Stronger. Wiser. More sure of yourself. The version of you who finally figured out how to stop living on autopilot. The you who wakes up excited, who isn't drowning in self-doubt, who doesn't let life just happen to them anymore.

That future you?

They're looking back at you right now, smiling.

Because they know something you don't yet: You're going to be okay. You're going to be more than okay.

I wish I could tell you that life gets easier, but the truth is, it doesn't.

What happens instead is that you get stronger. You get smarter. You stop taking yourself so seriously. You start choosing yourself.

And that's where everything changes.

This book is here for those nights when you feel like giving up.

For those mornings when you wake up wondering if anything will ever feel different.

For those moments when the world tells you you're not enough, and you need something to remind you that you are.

I'm writing this for you, but I'm also writing this for someone very special, my niece, Srinija.

She's only six now, but one day, she'll grow up and face the same questions we all do.

Who am I supposed to be?

What if I don't fit in?

How do I figure it all out?

And when that day comes, I hope she finds these pages.

I hope she realizes that life isn't about having all the answers, it's about being brave enough to keep asking the right questions.

And I hope she, and you, and anyone who picks up this book, understands one thing above all:

You're not alone.

You never were. You never will be.

Now let's rewrite the story together.
With love,
Pipi

Preface

Every time you think that the day cannot get worse than this or that life is so unfair— pick up this book. I promise you— you will be a whole new person by the end of it.

CHAPTER I

THE DOPAMINE DETOX THAT ACTUALLY WORKS

Alright, let's start with the truth. You don't need another preachy self-help book telling you to quit social media, delete Netflix, and spend your weekends staring at the ceiling in the name of a dopamine detox. You already know that endlessly scrolling Instagram at 2 AM while lying to yourself about sleeping early is not peak productivity. What you probably don't know is that dopamine isn't the enemy.

No, your brain is not broken. You are not addicted to your phone. You are simply **stuck in a loop of low-effort, low-reward distractions that trick your brain into thinking it's happy, when in reality, you're just... kind of okay.**

And okay is a terrible place to be.

This chapter is not about making your life boring in the name of self-improvement. It's about hacking the way dopamine actually works, so you can naturally feel excited, focused, and alive without having to do a damn thing that sounds like punishment.

So let's get into it.

Andrew Huberman Didn't Say This, But He Should Have

Neuroscientist Andrew Huberman talks a lot about dopamine. You might have heard his famous advice: "Stop bombarding your brain with quick hits of dopamine so you can restore its natural balance." But what most people miss is that dopamine isn't about pleasure—it's about pursuit.

Dopamine doesn't spike when you get what you want. It spikes when you're **chasing something exciting**. That's why a new project feels thrilling at first but boring once you actually have to do it. It's why falling in love is intoxicating, but long-term relationships take work. Your brain is literally designed to reward you for wanting, not for having.

Which means if you want a **dopamine detox that actually works**, you don't need to remove dopamine. You need to **stop overdosing on cheap dopamine and start feeding your brain the kind of dopamine that makes life feel like an adventure again.**

How do you do that? Simple. You replace the "easy hits" with dopamine sources that require effort.

And before you groan, let me introduce you to someone who hacked this way before Huberman made it cool.

Why Anthony Bourdain Had More Dopamine Than Any Tech Bro On Adderall

Let's talk about Anthony Bourdain. Yes, the legendary chef, traveler, and storyteller who lived a life so dopamine-rich it made everyone else's existence look like a grayscale version of The Truman Show.

Bourdain's entire career was built on **intense curiosity and voluntary discomfort**. He didn't just watch people eat exotic food—he jumped on a plane, went to their country, and ate things that made most people gag. He put himself in unfamiliar situations, surrounded himself with interesting people, and followed his obsessions like a bloodhound.

And that's why his brain was never bored.

Bourdain wasn't "detoxing" from dopamine. He was **hacking it** by giving his brain real adventure instead of cheap stimulation.

Most people try to break their bad habits by relying on willpower. That's stupid. Instead of quitting doomscrolling, you need to **replace it with something that makes your brain light up even more.**

This is why most dopamine detoxes fail—they remove the junk but don't replace it with anything fun.

Bourdain-level dopamine comes from three things:

1. **Chasing something new (even if it's small)**
2. **Doing things that scare you a little**
3. **Surrounding yourself with people who make life feel cinematic**

Now, I know what you're thinking. "Great, but I can't just book a flight to Vietnam and start eating cobra hearts."

Fair. So let's talk about how to do this without leaving your house.

The Stupidly Simple Trick That Makes Life Feel Like a Movie Again

Your brain is designed to respond to novelty. That's why the first time you drive a car, it's exhilarating, but by the 50th time, it's just another Tuesday. Your dopamine system gets bored if you don't give it something fresh.

The trick? **Micro-adventures.**

This is what keeps people like Richard Branson excited about life while everyone else is stuck in existential dread by age 30. He deliberately throws himself into **tiny, unpredictable situations** just to keep his brain sharp.

You can do this too. And no, it doesn't mean jumping out of a plane (unless you're into that). It means:

- Taking a different route to work.
- Ordering something on the menu you never would.
- Talking to a stranger in a way that's slightly out of character for you.
- Trying an activity you're convinced you'll suck at.
- Swapping your usual Netflix binge for a documentary about something you know nothing about.

Your brain **lives** for these little disruptions. It doesn't need a massive life overhaul. Just enough variety to keep it guessing.

Do this consistently, and suddenly, even your normal days will feel more alive.

How to Make Your Brain WorkForYou Instead of Against You

Here's another thing no one tells you: **Dopamine resets work best when you attach them to a larger mission.**

Elon Musk doesn't wake up excited because he's scrolling TikTok. He wakes up excited because he's trying to colonize Mars. His dopamine system is **locked onto a massive, impossible goal that forces his brain to stay engaged.**

Most people don't have that. They go through life reacting to whatever comes their way instead of actively

picking something to pursue.

Your mission doesn't have to be "change the world." It can be:

- "I want to build a side hustle that makes enough to quit my job."
- "I want to become so good at something that people start paying attention."
- "I want to say yes to things I'd usually avoid, just to see where it takes me."

If your brain has **nothing to chase, it will chase distractions.**

Now, before you go thinking this is all about chasing highs, let me tell you something crucial: **If you can't handle boredom, you'll always be stuck in a dopamine loop.**

The best performers such as athletes, artists, entrepreneurs—have one thing in common. **They are insanely good at being bored.**

Most people quit before they even start because the beginning of anything sucks. Learning a new skill is frustrating. Writing is slow. Working out feels pointless at first.

But if you can sit with the boredom instead of running to TikTok for a dopamine hit, something magical happens. Your brain adapts. Suddenly, that thing you hated? You start to enjoy it. You've rewired your dopamine system to crave effort instead of escape.

And once you do that? Game over. Life becomes fun again.

Why Boredom is the Secret Weapon No One Talks About

Here's something that will probably piss you off: **Boredom is not the enemy. It's actually the secret to rewiring your dopamine system.**

You know how little kids are constantly coming up with weird games, imaginary friends, or turning a cardboard box into a spaceship? That's because they're not overloading their brains with constant stimulation. Their brains **crave novelty, so they create it.**

Most adults never do this. The second there's even a hint of boredom, they grab their phone. Waiting in line? Scroll. Commercial break? Scroll. Lying in bed? Scroll.

And the more you avoid boredom, the worse your attention span gets. The worse your attention span gets, the harder it becomes to enjoy anything that **isn't instantly stimulating.**

But here's where it gets wild: **If you sit with boredom long enough, your brain will literally start rewiring itself to find excitement in whatever you're doing.**

This is why some of the greatest ideas in history came when people were bored out of their minds. Steve Jobs would take long, aimless walks. Albert Einstein worked a dull patent office job where he spent hours daydreaming. Bill Gates literally **locks himself in a cabin for a "think week" with zero distractions.**

So, if you're serious about a dopamine reset, **you have to reintroduce boredom into your life**—not as punishment, but as a catalyst.

Try this: **Next time you feel the urge to reach for your phone out of habit, don't.** Just sit with the discomfort for five minutes. Your brain will hate it at first. And then? It will start finding ways to entertain itself. **That's when the rewiring starts.**

What to Do Right Now (Because Waiting Till Tomorrow Is a Scam)

If you take one thing away from this chapter, let it be this:

- Stop trying to "detox" from dopamine like it's the enemy.
- Start replacing cheap dopamine with high-effort dopamine.
- Make tiny changes today—not next Monday, not "after this project."

And most importantly? Pick something to chase. Your brain is dying for a mission. Give it one.

Why Keanu Reeves Is the Most Dopamine-Rich Man in Hollywood

You know who has life completely figured out? **Keanu Reeves.**

He doesn't chase attention. He doesn't flex his wealth. He rides the subway, randomly donates millions of dollars, and disappears for months at a time without anyone knowing what he's up to.

But here's the kicker: **Keanu has mastered dopamine regulation.**

Most celebrities get addicted to external validation. They live for the rush of being famous, constantly seeking approval from fans and the media. Their dopamine systems are completely hijacked by social status.

Keanu? He gets his dopamine from **internal** sources. He creates, disappears, does whatever he finds meaningful, and doesn't care if the world is watching or not.

This is the **ultimate dopamine hack**—when your motivation comes from within, instead of from likes, views, or attention.

Want to be more like Keanu? Try this: **Do something awesome and tell no one about it.**

- Learn a skill.
- Improve your health.
- Create something just for yourself.

The less you rely on external dopamine hits, the more in control you become. And suddenly, you're not chasing validation—you're just **enjoying the process.**

How Music Can Rewire Your Brain in 30 Seconds

If you've ever been instantly transported to a memory just by hearing an old song, congratulations—you've experienced **dopamine-triggered time travel.**

Music is one of the fastest ways to rewire your dopamine system because it taps into **anticipation, reward, and nostalgia**all at once. Your brain releases dopamine **before** the beat drops, because it knows what's coming.

That's why music can make boring tasks feel fun. Ever tried cleaning your room in silence? Now try it while blasting your favorite playlist. Your brain perceives it as **two completely different experiences.**

This is why athletes use music before competing. Why movies feel empty without a soundtrack. Why a simple walk can turn into **a full-on main-character moment** just by wearing headphones.

Want to hack your dopamine instantly? **Curate a "dopamine playlist"**—songs that make you feel unstoppable, nostalgic, or energized. Play it while doing something difficult. Watch how fast your brain starts associating effort with excitement.

The Reason Why Some People Seem Unstoppable

Ever wonder why some people seem to **always be on a mission**? The kind of people who start projects, finish them, and move on to something even cooler without ever burning out?

It's because their dopamine system is **hooked on the chase, not the outcome.**

The biggest mistake most people make is **thinking dopamine is about getting what you want.** It's not. It's about the thrill of the pursuit.

That's why people who focus only on the **result** get depressed the moment they achieve it. They worked so hard to reach the top, only to realize... there's nothing left to chase.

Meanwhile, the people who stay excited about life? They **never stop setting new challenges for themselves.**

David Goggins, the guy who went from being overweight to becoming a Navy SEAL and ultramarathon runner, is a perfect example. **He trains his brain to crave the pain of the process.**

Goggins says: "When you think you're done, you're only at 40%." His entire mindset is based on **pushing past comfort and finding pleasure in the struggle itself.**

Want to rewire your brain like Goggins? **Stop setting goals with an endpoint.** Instead, focus on **becoming the kind of person who chases challenges for fun.**

The Secret Dopamine Hack Hidden in Video Games

Ever played a game for hours without realizing how much time passed? That's because video games **are designed to hijack your dopamine system perfectly.**

They give you:

- **Clear missions.** (You always know what you're working toward.)
- **Small, constant rewards.** (XP points, achievements, new levels.)
- **A sense of progress.** (Even failures teach you something.)

Now, imagine if your real life was set up like this.

Instead of mindlessly grinding through your days, you could **gamify** your goals:

- Set missions for yourself every week. (Example: Learn how to cook three new meals.)
- Track your progress visually. (A whiteboard, a journal, or even a simple notes app.)
- Reward yourself when you complete something meaningful.

The reason video games are addictive is because they **make progress feel rewarding.** If your life doesn't feel exciting, it's probably because you're not **noticing** your progress.

Fix that, and suddenly, everything becomes more engaging.

Stop Waiting for Motivation—It's Never Coming

Here's one last dopamine truth bomb before we wrap this chapter: **If you're waiting to feel motivated before taking action, you're going to be waiting forever.**

Motivation comes after action, not before.

Think about it. Have you ever not wanted to work out, but once you forced yourself to start, suddenly you felt unstoppable? That's dopamine kicking in.

Your brain rewards action with motivation—not the other way around.

So the next time you catch yourself saying, "I'll start when I feel ready," remind yourself:

- You're never going to feel ready.
- You don't need to feel motivated.
- You just need to start.

And once you start? That's when the dopamine kicks in, rewiring your brain to actually want to keep going.

See you in the next chapter, where we turn your existence into a full-blown **blockbuster movie.**

CHAPTER II

THE 'MAIN CHARACTER' PROTOCOL

If you've ever looked at your life and thought, "Why does my existence feel like a background scene in someone else's movie?"—congratulations. You're self-aware. That's the first step.

The second step? **Fixing it.**

Because here's the brutal truth: Nobody is coming to make your life more interesting for you. There's no secret director waiting in the wings, ready to hand you a better script. You are the writer, the producer, the star, and, most of the time, the biggest obstacle in your own story.

-The problem is, most people live like **NPCs** (non-playable characters, for those who never got addicted to video games). They exist in autopilot mode, moving from one thing to another, reacting instead of acting, waiting for a perfect moment that never comes.

Meanwhile, the people who seem to have the most insane, interesting, action-packed lives? They **decided** to be the main character. They built their own narratives instead of waiting for something cool to happen to them.

And that's what this chapter is about. **How to stop being an extra in your own life and start living like the protagonist.**

How Matthew McConaughey Wrote His Own Script (Literally and Metaphorically)

Before Matthew McConaughey became the deep-thinking, Lincoln-driving, Oscar-winning legend he is today,

Hollywood had him boxed into one role: **the rom-com guy.**

He was good at it, sure. But after a string of successful romantic comedies, McConaughey realized he was just playing the same character on repeat. He wasn't in control of his story—Hollywood was.

So, he did something insane.

At the peak of his career, he **quit acting for two years.** No new roles, no auditions, nothing.

People thought he was crazy. But he knew that as long as he kept saying yes to the same roles, he'd never break out of the mold. He had to create space for a better script.

And when he came back? He completely reinvented himself with True Detective, Interstellar, and Dallas Buyers Club—movies that showed his real range.

That's what being the main character is about. **You don't get to change your story until you stop accepting roles that don't serve you.**

Ask yourself:

- What are you saying "yes" to out of habit, not desire?
- What version of yourself are you stuck playing just because it's familiar?
- What's the role you actually want to step into?

Because the second you stop showing up for the script that isn't yours, the right one starts writing itself.

The Hemingway Trick: Turn Your Life into a Story Worth Telling

Ernest Hemingway wasn't just a legendary writer. He was a **main character on steroids.**

He fought in wars, survived plane crashes, drank absurd amounts of whiskey, ran with the bulls in Spain, and somehow still found time to write some of the greatest novels of all time.

But here's the wild part: He didn't wait for an interesting life to happen to him. He **deliberately designed it** to be worth writing about.

And you don't have to go to war or fight a bull to do the same.

The trick? **Start treating your life like it's a book you'd want to read.**

Hemingway's secret wasn't just that he lived adventurously. It was that he observed everything with the curiosity of a writer. He **paid attention to details, to people, to emotions.** He made even the smallest moments feel significant because he saw them through the lens of storytelling.

Try this:

- **Narrate your life in your head like it's a book.** Instead of thinking, "Ugh, another boring commute," reframe it: "The protagonist stepped onto the train, headphones in, mind brimming with ideas, unknowingly on the edge of something life-changing."
- **Start collecting experiences like a novelist.** Try things just so you have a story to tell later. It's a ridiculous but foolproof way to make your life feel more like an adventure.
- **Romanticize the mundane.** Hemingway could describe drinking a cup of coffee in a way that made it sound like a spiritual experience. Your life is already more interesting than you think—it just depends on how you frame it.

When you start viewing your life as a story in progress, you become more intentional about what happens next. And suddenly, everything feels a lot less random.

The Danny Ocean Effect: Assemble Your Cast

In Ocean's Eleven, George Clooney's character, Danny Ocean, pulls off an insane Vegas heist. But the most important part of the movie? He **picks the best crew.**

Every main character needs a supporting cast that makes them better. Yet most people surround themselves with **energy-draining, uninspiring, stuck-in-their-ways** people who keep them playing small.

Main characters don't do that. They **curate their cast.**

Want to level up your life instantly? **Audit your social circle.**

- Who are the people who make you feel **energized** after hanging out with them?
- Who actually **challenges** you instead of just agreeing with everything you say?
- Who is already living at the level you want to reach?

Start **actively seeking out** people who force you to think bigger. People who introduce you to new ideas, new opportunities, new ways of seeing the world.

And if your current cast is holding you back? Time for a rewrite.

Why Steve Jobs Had a Signature Look (And Why You Need One Too)

Steve Jobs wore the same black turtleneck and jeans every day. Not because he was boring, but because he knew that **having a signature style made him instantly recognizable.**

All great main characters have a **defining trait**—something that makes them stand out, something that makes people remember them.

This could be:

- A personal style (think Karl Lagerfeld's sunglasses or Anna Wintour's bob haircut).
- A catchphrase or way of speaking that becomes part of your identity.
- A specific talent, habit, or skill that makes people associate you with something unique.

When you create a signature element for yourself, you instantly become more memorable. And when you're memorable, opportunities start finding **you.**

The 'Say Yes, Then Figure It Out' Rule

Main characters don't sit around waiting for confidence. They **say yes first and worry about logistics later.**

Richard Branson, founder of Virgin, built his entire empire on this rule. One of his most famous quotes? "If someone offers you an amazing opportunity and you're not sure you can do it, say yes—then figure it out later."

Most people operate the opposite way. They wait until they feel ready, until they have all the answers, until conditions are perfect.

Guess what? That day **never comes.**

The fastest way to step into the main character role is to **start saying yes to things before you feel qualified.**

- Someone asks you to speak at an event? Say yes.
- A job opportunity comes up that feels slightly out of reach? Say yes.
- A new experience comes along that makes you nervous? Say yes.

The best main characters aren't fearless. They're just willing to jump before they're 100% ready.

Your Story is Already Happening—Start Writing It Better

You don't have to wait for a big break, a perfect moment, or a life-changing event to start living like the main character.

You just have to **decide** that your story is worth telling.

So start acting like it.

A lot of people walk through life like they're waiting for someone to hand them permission slips. Permission to speak up in a room. Permission to take a risk. Permission to stop playing small. But here's the uncomfortable truth: **Nobody is ever going to give you permission.**

Think of the most interesting people you know. The ones who always seem to have the best stories, the weirdest connections, the wildest opportunities landing in their laps. Are they the ones who sit quietly, waiting for the right time to make a move? No. They **act first, figure things out later.**

Because here's the secret: **People treat you the way you tell them to treat you.**

If you carry yourself like a background character—staying small, hesitating, waiting for someone to notice you—you'll be treated like one. If you walk into a room like you belong there, people will assume you do. If you introduce yourself with confidence, people will listen.

This is not about faking it. It's about **owning your space.**

Look at someone like **Quentin Tarantino.** This man had no formal film education. No industry connections. He worked at a video store, watching movies obsessively, teaching himself how to write scripts. And when he finally got his break, he didn't walk into Hollywood like a nervous newcomer. He walked in like he had something **worth paying attention to.**

And guess what? People paid attention.

If you start treating yourself like the main character, the world will adjust accordingly.

That means walking into situations like you belong—even if you don't fully believe it yet. It means speaking up even when your voice shakes. It means deciding that you are already worth listening to, before anyone else does.

Because confidence doesn't come from external validation. It comes from **acting like you deserve to be here, long before anyone else agrees.**

And speaking of showing up, let's talk about something most people never think about: **Main characters know how to make an entrance.**

Have you ever seen someone walk into a room and instantly command attention—not because they're loud or flashy, but because they just **have a presence?** That's not an accident.

Actors, public speakers, CEOs—they all know how to use **body language, energy, and timing** to make people notice them. And you don't have to be famous to do it.

Here's how:

- When you enter a space, **pause for half a second.** Don't rush in, don't shrink yourself. That small pause signals confidence.
- **Look around, not down.** Most people walk into a room glued to their phone or avoiding eye contact. The simple act of looking up, scanning the room, and acknowledging people makes you instantly more present.
- **Move with purpose.** Whether you're walking, sitting, or just standing, do it like you mean to be there. Fidgeting, crossing your arms, or shifting nervously makes you seem unsure—even if you're faking confidence, do it with full commitment.

There's a reason characters like James Bond or Olivia Pope (from Scandal) seem effortlessly powerful in every scene. **It's how they carry themselves.**

And once you start doing this, people will feel your presence before you even say a word.

Another thing main characters never do? **Explain themselves too much.**

Look at someone like **Greta Gerwig.** When she pitched Barbie, she didn't spend hours justifying why a movie about a plastic doll could be profound. She simply spoke about it with conviction, and people bought in.

Most people over-explain because they're secretly asking for permission. They don't trust that what they're saying is valuable, so they keep adding disclaimers, softening their words, waiting for someone to say, "Yes, you're right."

Main characters don't do that. They **state things as fact.**

Imagine the difference between these two sentences:

1. "I was thinking maybe we could try this idea, but totally up to you."
2. "I have an idea. Here's why it will work."

The second one commands respect. Not because it's pushy, but because it signals **certainty.**

And certainty is what makes people pay attention.

This is why some people can walk into a meeting and instantly get everyone's interest, while others struggle to be heard. It's not what they're saying—it's **how** they say it.

Try this for a week: **Stop over-explaining. Say what you mean, then stop talking. Let the silence do the work.**

Because here's the truth: **Main characters don't chase approval. They set the tone, and people follow.**

Now, let's address the one excuse that always comes up when people start thinking about rewriting their role in life: "But what if people don't like the new version of me?"

Here's the thing: **Not everyone is supposed to like you.**

In fact, if you start living like the main character and nobody gets uncomfortable, you're probably doing it wrong.

Look at someone like **Tyler, The Creator.** He built an entire career out of being unapologetically himself—loud, weird, boundary-pushing. Did people criticize him? Constantly. Did it stop him? Not once.

The people who resonate with your energy will find you. The ones who don't? They were never meant for you anyway.

And this is where most people fail. They start stepping into their main character energy, but the second someone raises an eyebrow or questions them, they shrink back. They start worrying about whether they're too much.

Listen: **You are always going to be "too much" for the wrong people. But you will be** exactly **right for the ones who matter.**

The goal is not to make everyone like you. The goal is to be so authentic, so **undeniably yourself,** that the right people can't help but notice.

This is why the best characters in books, movies, and real life **have an edge.** They are not neutral. They don't blend in.

And neither should you.

So starting now, you're done playing small. You're done waiting for permission. You're done living as a passive character in your own story.

You are the main character. **Act like it.**

CHAPTER III

THE 'ONE DEGREE OF CHAOS' RULE

It's time to get real.

If your life feels predictable, uninspiring, or like you're living on autopilot, it's probably because you are too damn comfortable.

Now, before you argue, let me clarify: Comfort is great when it comes to blankets, hoodies, and having a solid Wi-Fi connection. But when it becomes your default setting, your brain goes numb.

You ever notice how the first bite of cake is *mind-blowing*, but by the fourth, it's just... cake? That's your brain, constantly adapting. When everything in your life is familiar—your routine, your conversations, even your thoughts, it stops registering excitement.

The solution? Inject controlled chaos into your life, one small act at a time. Not in a self-destructive *let's quit my job and move to a commune* kind of way (unless that's your thing), but in a way that keeps your brain on its toes.

This is called the **One Degree of Chaos Rule.**

The idea? You don't need to flip your life upside down to make it exciting. You just need to tilt it slightly off balance, like a movie protagonist about to make a questionable but entertaining decision.

Richard Feynman Knew the Secret to Staying Excited About Life

Take Richard Feynman, one of the greatest physicists of all time. He was brilliant, sure, but he also had a habit of doing completely random things just to keep his brain fresh. He learned how to crack safes for fun. He played the bongos. He made a game out of figuring out how ants find food. Feynman didn't just study physics; he actively made sure his brain stayed curious about *everything*, because he knew that curiosity is what keeps life interesting.

And that's exactly why most people feel stuck. They stop being curious. They live like they already know how everything works. They go to the same places, eat the same meals, talk to the same people, and wonder why life has lost its edge.

So here's what you do: disrupt yourself in tiny, intentional ways. Order a meal you'd never normally choose. Walk somewhere instead of driving, even if it takes longer. Start a conversation with someone you'd usually ignore. Rearrange the furniture in your house. Watch a documentary on something you know absolutely nothing about. The goal isn't to create chaos for the sake of it—it's to *force your brain to wake up*.

Why Jim Carrey Wrote Himself a $10 Million Check

Jim Carrey is known for his comedy, but what most people don't realize is that he's also a master of self-disruption. Before he became famous, he wrote himself a check for $10 million for "acting services rendered" and dated it for the future. Then, instead of waiting for his big break, he **acted as if he had already made it.**

Carrey didn't just sit around waiting for his life to change—he *became* the person who would eventually cash that check. He took risks, did ridiculous performances, and put himself in situations that forced him to grow. He

created his own plot twist.

That's what controlled chaos looks like. It's putting yourself in a situation where you have no choice but to evolve.

The Tiny Chaos Hack That Keeps Life Interesting

The mistake most people make when they feel stuck is assuming they need some *big* change to shake things up. Quit their job. Move to another country. Buy a motorcycle and start a new life as a mysterious stranger. But huge changes don't always work because they're overwhelming. The brain panics and tries to reset back to comfort mode as soon as possible. That's why most dramatic life overhauls fail within months.

What actually works is **small, intentional acts of chaos**—tiny disruptions that force your brain to wake up without sending it into full-on panic mode. If you usually take the same route to work, take a different one. If you always order the same coffee, change it up. If you always go to the same grocery store, go to a completely different one on the other side of town. Sounds stupidly simple, right? But these tiny shifts force your brain to start paying attention again.

When you change something—even something minor, your brain can't predict what's coming next. And when it can't predict, it starts *noticing* again. Your senses sharpen. Time slows down. Life starts feeling *different*, even if nothing dramatic has changed.

Why You Need a Little Bit of 'Good Trouble'

Every great main character has a little bit of rebellion in them. They're not reckless, but they're also not blindly following the script that was handed to them. They question things. They poke at the edges of reality. They get into *just enough* trouble to make life feel interesting.

David Bowie was a walking embodiment of this rule. He never let himself become predictable—not to his audience, not to himself. He would change his entire persona the second he got too comfortable. He went from Ziggy Stardust to the Thin White Duke to whatever experimental version of himself he felt like playing next. His career lasted *decades* because he kept rewriting the story before anyone else could.

And this applies to confidence too. The people who seem the most fearless aren't necessarily born that way. They've just trained their brains to get comfortable with unpredictability. Take someone like Amelia Earhart. She wasn't born fearless. But she made a habit of deliberately pushing into new territory. She once took a job as a truck driver just because she wanted to know what it felt like.

How to Trick Your Brain into Loving Uncertainty

Here's the thing—most people avoid change because they associate uncertainty with anxiety. But your brain doesn't *have* to interpret it that way. It can just as easily associate uncertainty with **excitement**.

Ever notice how people who love roller coasters experience the exact same physical symptoms as people who hate them? The heart races, adrenaline pumps, muscles tense. But instead of interpreting it as fear, they register it as *fun*.

This is called **cognitive reappraisal,** your ability to *choose* how you interpret an event. And it works for everything.

If you keep telling yourself, *"Change is scary,"* your brain will believe you. But if you reframe uncertainty as a *plot twist,* something exciting, something leading to an unknown adventure—you'll start to crave it.

Start small. Try something slightly uncomfortable today, and before your brain has time to freak out, tell yourself: *This is the start of something interesting.*

Because nothing interesting ever happens in a life that stays predictable.

Jim Carrey once said that he realized the power of his mind when he drove up to Mulholland Drive every night, looked over Los Angeles, and visualized directors offering him roles that would change his life. This was before *Ace Ventura,* before *Dumb and Dumber,* before *The Truman Show.* He wasn't famous yet. He wasn't rich. But he imagined himself already being there, to the point where it started to feel *real.* He didn't wait for Hollywood to hand him a script. He **wrote his own damn story first.**

This is exactly what happens when you inject controlled chaos into your life. You start living as if something extraordinary is just around the corner, and before you know it, **it actually is.**

A lot of people get this wrong. They think the way to change their life is by making a vision board, setting some goals, and waiting for the universe to take care of the rest. But here's what they don't tell you—**the universe only starts working in your favor once you start shaking things up first.**

And shaking things up doesn't mean quitting your job overnight or making some drastic life-altering move that sends you into financial ruin. It means adding *just enough* unpredictability that your brain starts paying attention again. It means *just enough* discomfort to keep you evolving.

How David Lynch Uses Chaos to Fuel Creativity

If you ever feel stuck in a rut—creatively, mentally, or just in life in general—there is no better person to study than David Lynch. Lynch, the director behind *Twin Peaks* and *Mulholland Drive*, is known for making movies that feel like stepping into an alternate universe where nothing quite makes sense, but everything *feels* important.

His secret? He actively *seeks* the unknown.

Lynch has a practice he calls "catching the big fish." He believes that the best ideas—the ones that change your life—aren't just sitting there waiting for you. You have to go *fishing* for them. And the only way to do that is to break your usual patterns and force your mind into uncharted territory.

Most people, when they're stuck, try to think their way out of it. But thinking doesn't work when you're in a loop. You need *new input*. You need **randomness**. You need to go somewhere you wouldn't normally go, talk to people you wouldn't normally talk to, and expose yourself to things that don't immediately make sense.

Lynch once spent hours just staring at **a dead fish on the beach** because he was fascinated by the way it was decomposing. He wasn't looking for a creative breakthrough. He was just training his brain to notice *everything*. And that's what great storytellers, artists, and innovators do—they **pay attention to things that other**

people ignore.

You don't need to stare at a dead fish to shake up your brain, but you *do* need to start paying attention to things you'd normally overlook.

- Read a book about something you think you'd hate.
- Walk into a store you'd never shop at just to see what's inside.
- Pick a random object in your house and challenge yourself to notice something new about it.

The more you train your brain to see *everything*, the more interesting your life becomes.

The 'Stranger Conversation' Challenge

Want to instantly level up your ability to handle uncertainty? Talk to a stranger today. I don't mean a forced, awkward conversation about the weather—I mean actually engaging with someone you'd usually ignore.

This might sound small, but it's one of the fastest ways to rewire your brain for confidence. Most people go through life avoiding eye contact with cashiers, standing in corners at parties, and making every interaction as *transactional* as possible. But the main characters in life—the ones who always seem to attract opportunities, friendships, and once-in-a-lifetime experiences? They **engage** with the world.

Matthew McConaughey once told a story about how he landed one of his first big acting roles just by **talking to the right stranger at the right time.** He wasn't even auditioning. He was just at a bar, being his usual charismatic self, and the next thing he knew, he was in

Dazed and Confused.

It's not magic. It's math. The more you put yourself in situations where randomness can happen, the more likely something cool *will* happen.

So today, say something unexpected to someone. Compliment the person behind you in line at the grocery store. Ask a cab driver about the weirdest passenger they've ever had. If you're feeling bold, walk into a café and start a conversation with the most interesting-looking person there. Worst case scenario, you learn something new. Best case? Your life changes a little.

Why Most People Will Never Escape Their Routine (And How Not to Be One of Them)

The reason most people never get out of their own way is because they build routines that become *too* rigid. They create a comfort zone so perfectly designed that they forget to ever step outside of it.

Take Nikola Tesla. He was a literal genius, but toward the end of his life, he became *too* attached to his routines. He only ate certain foods. He followed an extreme sleeping schedule. He limited his interactions. And by the time he died, he had faded into obscurity—outsmarted not by lack of intelligence, but by his refusal to adapt.

Compare that to someone like Elon Musk, who constantly disrupts *his own* life on purpose. He'll switch industries overnight, take risks most people wouldn't even *consider*, and challenge himself with problems so big that his brain *has*to stay engaged. Love him or hate him, the guy is a walking dopamine reset.

This is why *small* disruptions matter. You don't have to launch a rocket to break out of a rut. You just have to make sure you're not *repeating* the same day over and over again.

- If your Monday looks exactly like your Thursday, change something.
- If you're eating the same meals, switch it up.
- If your social circle never introduces you to new ideas, expand it.

Your brain *wants* to explore. It just needs permission.

How to Trick Your Brain into Craving the Unknown

Your brain is wired to seek comfort, but it's also wired to chase **novelty**. The trick is to convince it that uncertainty isn't scary—it's exciting.

Here's a wild fact: **The chemical reaction in your brain when you're scared is the exact same as when you're excited.** Your heart races. Your adrenaline spikes. The only difference is the **story you tell yourself** about what's happening.

That's why people who love roller coasters experience the same physiological response as people who hate them—their bodies are doing the same thing, but their *brains* interpret it differently.

If you can train yourself to reframe **uncertainty as excitement,** you will become unstoppable.

- Next time you feel nervous about doing something new, literally say out loud, *"I'm excited."*
- If a situation feels unfamiliar, remind yourself: *This is a plot twist, not a disaster.*

- When faced with an opportunity that scares you, ask: *If this was a movie, what would the main character do?*

You don't need to be reckless. You don't need to burn your life to the ground just to feel something. You just need **one degree of chaos**—just enough to make sure you're still awake.

Because the alternative?

A life that feels like it's on repeat, forever. And you deserve better than that.

CHAPTER IV

THE REVERSE BUCKET LIST HACK

If you've ever made a bucket list, chances are you filled it with the usual suspects—skydiving, visiting the Eiffel Tower, maybe even writing a book or learning a new language. That's cute. But also completely **backward**.

Because here's the real question: **How many of the things on your list are actually yours?**

Not things you added because they sound impressive. Not things you stole from some Pinterest board called "100 Things to Do Before You Die". Not things your parents, friends, society, or some hyper-optimized self-improvement guru convinced you should be your goals.

I'll wait.

Most people don't have a bucket list. They have a **socially acceptable checklist of achievements** they think will make them happy. But happiness doesn't come from adding more things to do before you die. It comes from **deleting the things you never actually cared about in the first place.**

This is where the **Reverse Bucket List Hack** comes in. Instead of making a list of what you want to do, we're going to make a list of what you **don't** want to do—so you can clear out the mental clutter and actually focus on the things that set your brain on fire.

Why Your Goals Might Be Sabotaging You

Let's talk about Derek Sivers. The guy started CD Baby, made millions, then sold his company, gave most of the money away, and started living out of a backpack. Why? Because he realized half the stuff he was chasing wasn't even making him happy.

He created a rule called **"Hell Yeah or No"**—if something isn't a hell yeah, it's a no. Simple, brutal, effective. Because most people don't fail because they lack ambition. They fail because they're drowning in **too many things they feel obligated to do.**

Ever wonder why billionaires wear the same outfit every day? It's not just for aesthetics. It's because every decision—no matter how small—takes up mental space. And when your brain is full of **goals that aren't yours**, you burn energy chasing things that leave you exhausted instead of fulfilled.

So before we talk about what you should be doing, let's first clear out the **garbage goals** that are secretly ruining your dopamine system.

The Five-Minute Reverse Bucket List Exercise

This is going to be uncomfortable. Which means you **need** to do it.

1. Grab a piece of paper or open your notes app.
2. Write down **every single goal, dream, or thing you've ever thought you "should" do.** Travel to Japan. Get a six-pack. Start a YouTube channel. Whatever is floating around in your subconscious. Write. It. All. Down.
3. Now, **go through each item and ask yourself:** If no one ever knew I did this, would I still want to do it?

4. The ones that feel like an **immediate, guilt-free no**? **Cross them out.**

Boom. You just saved yourself **years** of wasted effort. Now let's go deeper.

Why Most People Are Addicted to the Wrong Pursuits

Ever heard of the **arrival fallacy**? It's a psychological phenomenon where you think achieving a goal will make you happy, but once you get there, it's just... meh.

This is why some people climb the corporate ladder for years, finally get the corner office, and then stare out the window thinking, This is it?

Or why celebrities hit peak fame, realize it doesn't fix their inner demons, and spiral into existential crises.

It's because **they never wanted the thing itself. They wanted the feeling they thought it would give them.**

Happiness isn't about having more. It's about **pursuing the right things for the right reasons.**

So if you've ever felt like you're grinding toward something that should make you happy but isn't, this is your sign to **opt out.**

This is what **Marie Kondo did for physical clutter**, but we're doing it for your life.

The Science of Why Less is More

Harvard psychologist Daniel Gilbert ran a study where he found that people who **commit to fewer things are actually happier.** Why? Because when you spread your focus across too many ambitions, you **never fully**

experience any of them. You're always half-in, half-out. Your brain is constantly distracted by what's next instead of enjoying what's now.

Minimalism isn't just about decluttering your closet. It's about decluttering your **mental real estate.**

So if you've ever felt overwhelmed, burnt out, or like life is speeding by without you actually feeling it, the problem isn't that you need to do more. It's that you need to **do less, better.**

How to Create a Life That Feels Like Yours (Instead of a Group Project)

Once you've slashed all the fake goals, you need to **rebuild your list from scratch**—but this time, using **your actual desires, not society's expectations.**

Here's how:

1. **Think back to the last time you lost track of time doing something.** What were you doing? That's a clue.
2. **What did you obsess over as a kid?** That's another clue.
3. **If you had a year off with unlimited money, how would you spend your time?** The answer **isn't** about money—it's about what actually excites you when obligations are removed.

The goals that survive **this** test? Those are the ones worth chasing.

Why You Should Delete the Word "Should" From Your Vocabulary

Jim Carrey once said, "Your need for acceptance can make you invisible in this world." The second you start chasing things because you think you should, you start fading into the background of your own life.

So from now on, every time you catch yourself saying, "I should do this", replace it with, "Do I actually want to?"

Most of the time, the answer is no. And when you stop doing things out of obligation, you make room for the **things that actually make you feel alive.**

The One-Week Experiment That Will Change Your Life

I want you to do something ridiculous for the next seven days.

1. Say **no** to something you'd normally say yes to out of obligation.
2. Say **yes** to something purely because it excites you.
3. If something feels like it's draining your energy, **cut it off without over-explaining.**

Then just observe.

See how it feels to stop living for external validation and start living on your terms.

People might be confused at first. They might ask what's wrong with you. That's a good sign. That means you're disrupting the pattern.

Because most people will live their whole lives checking boxes they didn't even choose. But **you're not most people.**

You're actually here, doing the work.

So rip up that old bucket list, and let's start making a new one. One that actually belongs to you.

Jim Carrey's story isn't just about success—it's about **walking away from the wrong game entirely.**

In his early years, Carrey did what every aspiring comedian was supposed to do. He worked the stand-up circuit, played by the industry's rules, and tried to fit into the mold of what Hollywood expected. He was desperate to be liked. He **wanted** approval.

So many of us choose our path out of fear disguised as practicality, he said in a speech at Maharishi University. What we really want seems impossibly out of reach, so we never dare to ask the universe for it.

Carrey wasn't just talking about success—he was talking about **freedom**. The freedom to stop chasing things just because they're expected of you. The freedom to quit the exhausting game of trying to be everything for everyone.

And the second he dropped the need for validation? His career exploded. He stopped playing it safe. He leaned into his weirdness. He wrote himself that now-famous $10 million check for "acting services rendered" before he ever made a dime in Hollywood. And within a few years, he was cashing real checks in that exact amount.

He **deleted** the version of success that wasn't his. And that's what set him free.

This is the power of **opting out**. We think success is about adding things—more goals, more accomplishments, more experiences—but the truth is, success is just as much about what you don't do.

Leonardo da Vinci understood this better than most people. Despite being one of history's greatest polymaths, Da Vinci actually quit more projects than he finished. He famously left paintings incomplete, abandoned ideas midway through, and constantly refined what was worth his time. The Mona Lisa? That was a **side project** he worked on sporadically for years, never obsessing over finishing it for the sake of completion. He wasn't chasing productivity—he was chasing what truly fascinated him.

Most of us don't have a problem with ambition. We have a problem with **wasting ambition on the wrong things.**

It's because **they never wanted the thing itself. They wanted the feeling they thought it would give them.**

Happiness isn't about having more. It's about **pursuing the right things for the right reasons.**

Think about Andre Agassi. One of the greatest tennis players of all time. Eight Grand Slam titles. Millions of dollars in prize money. A career most athletes dream of.

And he **hated every second of it.**

In his memoir Open, Agassi confessed that he never actually wanted to play tennis—he was forced into it by his father. Every win, every title, every record shattered was just another moment of waiting for happiness that never came.

He was wildly successful. And wildly miserable.

Because success means nothing if it's built on a foundation of obligations and expectations rather than genuine passion.

Let's talk about Keanu Reeves. The man is **Hollywood's greatest anomaly.**

In an industry obsessed with status, he doesn't care about fame. He doesn't live in a massive mansion. He takes the subway. He donates most of his earnings. He disappears for months at a time, then resurfaces with another legendary role—always on **his own terms.**

Why? Because Keanu **opted out** of the Hollywood game. He didn't let his success trap him in a cycle of trying to stay relevant, chasing awards, or proving anything to anyone. He figured out what mattered to him, and he **deleted everything else.**

And because he's so free from needing attention, people are obsessed with him. Ironically, **the people who chase success the least are often the ones who get it the most.**

Here's where people get stuck. They assume that opting out means giving up. That not chasing every goal means settling for less. But it's the opposite. It's about **making space for what actually matters.**

If you're overwhelmed, exhausted, or feel like you're working hard but not getting anywhere, **you don't need more motivation. You need subtraction.**

Here's your experiment for the week.

1. Say **no** to something you'd normally say yes to out of obligation.
2. Say **yes** to something purely because it excites you.
3. If something feels like it's draining your energy, **cut it off without over-explaining.**

Then just observe.

See how it feels to stop living for external validation and start living on your terms.

People might be confused at first. They might ask what's wrong with you. That's a good sign. That means you're disrupting the pattern.

Because most people will live their whole lives checking boxes they didn't even choose. But **you're not most people.**

You're actually here, doing the work.

So rip up that old bucket list, and let's start making a new one. One that actually belongs to you.

CHAPTER V

THE ART OF UNFORGETTABLE THEFT

The first time Pablo Picasso said, *"Good artists copy, great artists steal,"* people probably thought he was just being an arrogant little shit. But he wasn't talking about plagiarism. He was talking about **the secret behind every great creator, innovator, and thinker in history**—the art of **stealing like a genius.**

Because here's a fact that might ruin every romanticized idea you have about creativity: **Nothing is original.**

Every book, every song, every business idea, every TED Talk, every billion-dollar startup? **Recycled. Borrowed. Reassembled. Stolen from somewhere.** The people who change the world aren't the ones who sit around trying to come up with something completely new. They're the ones who know how to **take existing ideas and make them so undeniably their own that nobody questions where they came from.**

And yet, most people don't do this. Not because they can't, but because they're stuck in **imposter syndrome hell**—that little voice in their head whispering, *Who do you think you are?*

You know who didn't have that voice? Steve Jobs.

The Time Steve Jobs Shamelessly Stole His Best Ideas

Apple is one of the most iconic brands of all time. But here's something Apple diehards don't like to talk about: Steve Jobs didn't invent most of what made Apple successful.

In 1979, Jobs visited the **Xerox PARC research lab**, where he saw something revolutionary—**the graphical user interface.** Before this, computers were just ugly text-based command lines. No icons, no mouse, no visual anything. Xerox had basically built the first version of what would become Windows and macOS, but they didn't know what to do with it.

Jobs did.

He straight-up **stole** the idea and ran with it. By the time the Macintosh launched in 1984, Apple had completely outshined Xerox in the personal computer market. Xerox had the invention. Jobs had the **vision**.

That's the difference between a good artist and a great one. A good artist asks for permission. A great one **sees the potential, takes it, and transforms it into something new.**

So if you've ever hesitated to start something because you're worried it's "been done before," congratulations. You're right. **It has.** But nobody has done it **your way.**

Why Shakespeare Was the Biggest Thief of Them All

We treat Shakespeare like some divine literary genius, but the guy was **the original remix artist.**

Most of his plays? **Not original stories.**

- *Romeo and Juliet?* Stolen from an old Italian poem.
- *Hamlet?* Based on an ancient Norse legend.

- *Macbeth*? Inspired by real Scottish history.

What Shakespeare did wasn't create something from thin air—he took old stories, injected his own voice, twisted the narratives, added drama, and made them **better.**

And that's what you should be doing. **Stop waiting for some divine bolt of inspiration. Start stealing smarter.**

The Rule of the Three Thieves: How to Steal Like a Genius Without Feeling Like a Fraud

Great artists and thinkers don't just copy—they steal strategically. Here's how.

1. Steal from multiple sources at once

If you steal from one person, it's copying. If you steal from ten, it's research. If you steal from fifty, it's innovation.

Kanye West built his entire music career on **sampling**. He didn't just take one influence—he combined obscure soul records, 80s synth pop, gospel choirs, classical music, and turned them into something nobody had ever heard before.

The same applies to any kind of creative work. Business ideas? Mash up two industries. Writing? Study multiple genres and blend styles. The more sources you pull from, the more *undeniably yours* your work becomes.

2. Change at least 30% of what you steal

A good thief doesn't just take—they modify. When Tarantino "borrows" from old movies, he doesn't just recreate them shot-for-shot. He **changes enough to make them feel fresh.**

If you're copying something outright, you're doing it wrong. But if you're taking an idea and **mutating it** into something that only *you* could come up with? Now you're innovating.

3. Make it look effortless

The best thieves don't get caught because they **own** their work. They don't over-explain. They don't feel guilty. They present it with so much confidence that people don't even question where it came from.

Banksy, the anonymous street artist, once said: *"Art should comfort the disturbed and disturb the comfortable."* That's exactly what great thieves do—they don't just replicate what's safe. They **push it further.**

How to Destroy Imposter Syndrome in Five Minutes

You might be thinking, *Okay, fine, but what if I still feel like a fraud?*

Let's kill that thought. Right now.

Step 1: Look at every successful person in history

You know what you'll notice? **None of them were "ready" when they started.**

Maya Angelou once said, *"I have written eleven books, but each time I think, 'Uh oh, they're going to find out now. I've run a game on everybody.'"*

Even the legends feel like imposters. The difference is, **they don't let it stop them.**

Step 2: Realize that originality is a myth

There's nothing left to invent. Every "new" idea is just an old one wearing better clothes. Even Einstein's theory of relativity? **Built on the work of physicists before him.**

The sooner you accept that **stealing and remixing is how progress happens**, the sooner you'll stop feeling guilty about it.

Step 3: Start before you're ready

The biggest mistake people make? **Waiting to feel "qualified."** But you don't need permission. You don't need validation. You need **momentum.**

Here's a **quick five-minute hack** to prove it to yourself.

1. Pick something you've been putting off—starting a blog, making a video, launching a business idea.
2. Set a timer for five minutes.
3. Start working on it **immediately.** No planning, no overthinking, no researching. Just **do the thing**.

By the time the five minutes are up, you'll have proof that **you didn't need permission to begin with.**

Why the Future Belongs to the Best Thieves

The people who will succeed in the next decade aren't the ones waiting for a *completely original* idea. They're the ones who know how to **steal better, remix faster, and execute with more confidence.**

Look at Elon Musk. Tesla didn't invent the electric car. SpaceX didn't invent rockets. Neuralink didn't invent brain-computer interfaces. Musk is just **really good at stealing ideas from different industries and making them bigger than anyone else could.**

Or take Instagram. Before it became the app we know today, it was called **Burbn**—a cluttered mess of check-ins, gaming elements, and filters. Then the founders realized people only cared about **one** feature: the photos. So what did they do? **They stole the best part of their own app, killed the rest, and turned it into a billion-dollar company.**

That's what great thieves do. They **cut the fluff and focus on what actually works.**

So if you've been waiting for a sign to start, here it is.

Stop overthinking. Start stealing. Make it **so good, no one even questions where it came from.**

There's an old story about a young blacksmith, restless and eager, who spent his days in a forge filled with the sound of hammers striking metal. He was obsessed with creating something no one had ever seen before—**a sword so powerful that kings would fight wars just to wield it.**

He studied every blacksmith in the village, watched their techniques, memorized their secrets. But everything he made still felt... ordinary.

So he set off on a journey. He traveled through mountains where ancient monks crafted blades said to cut through stone. He ventured to the deserts where nomads whispered about metals that could channel the energy of the sun. He spent years in foreign lands, learning, stealing techniques, experimenting, **failing more times than he could count.**

And then, one day, he returned home. But instead of forging a completely new blade, he **took pieces of everything he had learned**—the balance of the monks' swords, the flexibility of the desert metals, the precision of his village's finest craftsmanship.

The result? **The perfect sword.**

And when people saw it, they didn't say, *Oh, he just combined a bunch of old techniques.*

They said, *Where did this magic come from?*

Because here's the thing—no one cared that he didn't invent sword-making from scratch. They only cared that he created something so **undeniably good** that it felt like magic.

The Universe Has Been Doing This Forever

This story isn't just about the blacksmith. It's about how **everything in the universe works.**

Think about evolution. No species on Earth **started from scratch.** Every living thing—every bird, every fish, every human—is a remix of what came before it. DNA itself is just **a long, glorified game of copy-paste, with a few tweaks along the way.**

The most successful mutations? They **weren't brand new**; they were just slight improvements on what was already there. The cheetah didn't appear out of nowhere—it evolved from slower ancestors, each generation "stealing" the fastest traits until it became the fastest land animal alive.

The same thing happens in the stars. A dying star doesn't just disappear—it explodes, spreading its elements across the galaxy. The **iron in your blood**? That came from an ancient star that exploded billions of years ago. The atoms that make up **everything you are,** they're **stolen from the universe itself.**

This is the law of reality: **Everything builds on something else. Nothing is truly original.**

So why do we think we have to be?

The Science of Why Stealing Works Better Than Starting From Scratch

Your brain **loves** stealing. It's literally wired to do it.

Every time you learn something new, your brain **doesn't create knowledge from scratch**—it takes existing neural pathways and **modifies them** to fit new information. That's why the best way to learn something isn't by memorizing textbooks, it's by connecting what you're learning to something you already know.

This is why **metaphors work.** Your brain doesn't know what a "concept" is until it links it to something **familiar.** That's why Einstein, when explaining relativity, didn't just drop a bunch of equations. He used metaphors like, *"Put your hand on a hot stove for a minute, and it seems like an hour. Sit with a pretty girl for an hour, and it seems like a minute."*

Your brain took that comparison and *stole* the logic behind it. Now, you understand relativity **without even realizing you learned it.**

This is also why your best ideas don't come when you're trying to be original. They come **when you're making connections between things that already exist.**

The internet itself? **A remix of old ideas.** The telephone + radio waves = the first mobile phone. GPS? **A remix of Einstein's theories + satellite technology.**

Even the way music is made today? **Pure remixing.** There's a reason why almost every pop song follows the same four chords—because those chords **already work.** Producers like Kanye West, Rick Rubin, and Pharrell **built entire careers on sampling, flipping, and reinventing old music.**

The Universe Rewards the Best Thieves

Let's go back to the blacksmith.

The reason his sword became legendary wasn't because he invented an entirely new way to make metal. It was because he **combined existing techniques in a way no one had before.**

And this is what separates the people who **stay stuck in self-doubt** from the people who actually build something.

The ones who get stuck? They're waiting to be "original." They're terrified of being accused of copying. They think if an idea *already* exists, it's too late for them to do anything with it.

But the ones who **actually create something valuable?** They understand that **originality is just invisible theft.**

They take from their influences, but they tweak. They adapt. They make it their own. And by the time they're done, no one even *questions* where the idea came from.

Because at the end of the day, **people don't care if something has been done before. They only care if it's done well.**

So steal. Remix. Borrow from history. Take what works and discard what doesn't. Because the universe **doesn't reward the person who waits for a completely original idea.**

It rewards the person **who takes the best ideas and makes them better.**

CHAPTER VI

THE 'GHOST TOWN' METHOD

Imagine you wake up tomorrow and **everyone you know has disappeared**. No social media. No texts. No one around to judge your choices, question your moves, or make passive-aggressive comments about your life. It's just you, alone, in a ghost town.

Now ask yourself: **What would you do differently?**

Would you still chase the same goals? Would you still dress the way you do? Would you still be working on what you're working on now? Or would you finally admit to yourself that half the decisions you make aren't yours at all?

Because let's be honest, most people don't make decisions. They **react to expectations**.

The job they choose? Influenced by their parents.
The lifestyle they have? Shaped by their friends.
The opinions they hold? Borrowed from Twitter.

And this is exactly why **most people stay stuck**. They never sit in silence long enough to actually hear what they want.

This is why billionaires, top athletes, and elite thinkers don't make decisions the way normal people do. **They shut out the noise first.**

The Reason Warren Buffett Never Listens to 99% of People

Warren Buffett is worth over $100 billion, and yet, his decision-making process is **the complete opposite of what**

you'd expect from someone that powerful.

He doesn't surround himself with more opinions. He doesn't consult a hundred experts before making a move. Instead, **he spends hours sitting alone in a quiet room, just thinking.**

Buffett calls this "going into his own ghost town." He actively **avoids** outside influence when making high-stakes decisions because he knows that **the more voices you let in, the harder it is to hear your own.**

In a world where people are drowning in advice, opinions, and 50 different articles telling them how to live, Buffett figured out the secret: **Most people don't need more input. They need less.**

Because here's the ugly truth—**the people you let influence you? They're usually just projecting their own fears.**

Want to quit your job and start something new? Someone will tell you it's risky—because they're scared of taking risks.
Want to move to a new city? Someone will say it's a bad idea—because they can't imagine leaving their comfort zone.
Want to chase an unconventional dream? Someone will say it's unrealistic—because they gave up on theirs.

And if you let these voices control you, you end up living someone else's ghost town instead of building your own.

The Science of Why Overthinking Kills Decision-Making

Harvard researchers found that **people who have too many choices end up making worse decisions.** It's called

decision fatigue, and it's why Steve Jobs wore the same black turtleneck every day. He didn't want to waste mental energy on deciding what to wear when he had bigger things to focus on.

Your brain has a limited amount of high-quality decisions it can make in a day. Every extra piece of information, every extra opinion, every extra choice? It drains that battery.

This is why billionaires **eliminate distractions before making decisions**. Jeff Bezos doesn't attend endless meetings. Mark Zuckerberg literally reduced his wardrobe to t-shirts and hoodies. Barack Obama said he only wore blue or gray suits during his presidency because he didn't want to waste time deciding what to wear.

They all know one thing that most people don't—**great decisions don't come from thinking harder. They come from creating an environment where you can think clearly.**

How to Apply the 'Ghost Town' Method in 5 Minutes

Here's how you can use this method today:

1. **Go somewhere quiet.** No phone, no music, no input from the outside world. Sit alone for just five minutes.
2. **Pick a decision you've been overthinking.** Career move? Relationship choice? Life direction? Choose one.
3. **Imagine the world has gone silent.** No opinions. No expectations. No one watching. If nobody would judge you, **what would you choose?**

You'll notice something strange—the answer usually comes faster than you expect. Not because you just figured it out, but because **you knew all along.** You were just letting too much noise drown it out.

Why The Most Successful People Say No More Than They Say Yes

If you study ultra-successful people, you'll notice something bizarre: **They reject way more opportunities than they accept.**

Warren Buffett once said, "The difference between successful people and really successful people is that really successful people say no to almost everything."

Why? Because the more you say yes, the more **other people start controlling your time.** And once you let that happen, you stop making your own decisions.

Most people don't struggle with not having enough opportunities. They struggle with **being too distracted by the wrong ones.**

Saying yes to a mediocre job means saying no to time spent finding a great one.

Saying yes to obligations you hate means saying no to your own priorities.

Saying yes to every invite, every favor, every pointless task? That's how you wake up ten years from now wondering where your life went.

The most powerful decision you can make isn't what to say yes to. It's **what to cut out.**

How 'Ghost Town' Thinking Can Make You Instantly Smarter

Here's a trick that will instantly boost your intelligence: **Before making a big decision, write down every influence that could be affecting it.**

Your boss? Your parents? Society's definition of success? Your fear of failing? Write them all down. Now, ask yourself: **Would I still make the same decision if none of these pressures existed?**

Most of the time, the answer is **no**.

And that's your red flag. It means you were never making the decision for yourself in the first place.

The real geniuses in the world aren't necessarily smarter than you. They just have **fewer influences pulling them in the wrong direction.**

The Hidden Superpower of Not Giving a F* What Others Think

There's a reason why the most iconic people in history—the Elon Musks, the Oprahs, the Richard Bransons—seem almost **delusional** at times.

It's because they **trained their brain to ignore irrelevant opinions.**

Elon Musk was laughed at when he started Tesla. They told him electric cars would never take off.
Oprah was told she wasn't "fit for television."
Richard Branson was told Virgin Airlines was a dumb idea that would fail within a year.

If they had let those voices control them, **they never would have changed the world.**

And neither will you—unless you learn how to filter out the noise.

The Ghost Town Challenge: Try It Right Now

1. **Pick something you've been hesitating on.** A risk you want to take. A change you want to make.
2. **Remove every external influence from the equation.** Pretend the world is empty. No judgment. No expectations. No one watching.
3. **Decide based on instinct, not fear.** The real answer is already inside you. You've just been too distracted to hear it.

The people who make the biggest impact aren't the ones who seek approval. They're the ones who **make their move before anyone else can tell them not to.**

So before you ask for another opinion, before you second-guess yourself into oblivion, ask this instead:

If nobody was watching, what would I do?

Now go do that.

Rumi once wrote, "Why do you stay in prison when the door is so wide open?"

Most people never realize they're in a prison because the walls are invisible. The bars aren't real. The lock isn't even there. The prison is made of opinions, social pressure, and the fear of what will happen if they decide to walk out.

That's why the **Ghost Town Method** is so powerful. It forces you to see what's been keeping you inside that imaginary prison all along. The second you strip away the noise, the expectations, the invisible pressures that have been shaping your decisions, you suddenly see how much of your life has been designed by people who don't have to live it.

And the people who escape? They don't necessarily have more talent, more intelligence, or more opportunities. They just **realize earlier than most that the walls were never real to begin with.**

How the Samurai Made Decisions Without Fear

The samurai of ancient Japan had a rule: **Every decision must be made within seven breaths.**

They believed that hesitation was the enemy of strength, that thinking too much about a choice would invite fear, doubt, and weakness. If you couldn't decide within seven breaths, it meant you were already losing control.

Modern psychology actually backs this up. Studies have shown that **the longer you take to make a decision, the more likely you are to overanalyze, hesitate, and default to the safest option rather than the best one.**

But the samurai didn't just trust speed, they also had a trick for eliminating fear entirely.

They practiced something called **"dying before going into battle."** They would sit in silence and **imagine their own death in the most detailed way possible,** not as a morbid exercise, but as a way to make peace with it. Because once they had accepted the worst possible outcome, fear no longer controlled them.

That's the kind of clarity you get when you remove external influence. When you stop making decisions based on what might go wrong, what people might say, or how you'll be judged, and you just **choose what actually makes sense for you.**

How to Use the Samurai Trick Right Now

Let's say you're stuck between two choices:

- Take a new opportunity that excites you but also terrifies you
- Stay in your current situation because it's comfortable and predictable

Most people will start analyzing. They'll make lists. They'll ask ten different people for their opinions. They'll wait for a **sign from the universe,** which is usually just a fancy way of saying I want an excuse to stay where I am.

The samurai would say: **Decide within seven breaths.**

If you had no one to consult, no one watching, no one to impress, **which choice would you make?**

That's your answer.

And if fear is stopping you? Do what the samurai did.

Imagine the worst possible outcome. Make peace with it. Ask yourself, Even if this fails completely, would I still want to try?

Because here's the truth, if you can accept the worst-case scenario and **it's still worth it**, you've already won.

Why the Most Legendary Thinkers Loved Isolation

Throughout history, the people who changed the world weren't the ones who were **constantly plugged in** to conversations, debates, and opinions. They were the ones who **intentionally disappeared** to think for themselves.

Nietzsche would take long, isolated walks in the mountains for hours before writing a single word.
Virginia Woolf insisted on having a "room of one's own" so she could create without distraction.
Nikola Tesla spent entire days alone in his New York hotel room, visualizing inventions before he ever built them.

They understood something that most people today have forgotten—**your mind is not designed to be in constant input mode.**

Right now, your brain is like a web browser with fifty tabs open. Social media. News. Family opinions. Career expectations. Some random argument you saw online that doesn't even involve you, but now it's taking up space in your head.

And yet, you wonder why it's hard to make decisions.

How to Build Your Own Mental Ghost Town

If you want the kind of clarity that billionaires, samurai, and philosophers have mastered, you have to **create space for it.**

- **One hour a week: No outside influence.** No social media. No texts. No conversations about your choices. Just you, sitting with your own thoughts.
- **Make one decision entirely alone.** No consulting. No second opinions. No input from anyone else. Trust your gut and go with it.
- **Mute the voices you hear the most.** If you always turn to the same friends, mentors, or media sources for advice, take a break from them and see what your own brain comes up with.

At first, it'll feel uncomfortable. Your brain will crave outside validation. It'll want someone to reassure you that you're making the "right" decision.

But after a while, something incredible happens—you **realize you never needed permission to begin with.**

The Hidden Truth About 'Bad' Decisions

People fear making the wrong choice because they think a bad decision will **ruin their life.** But unless you're gambling your entire existence on a single move, the truth is, most "bad" decisions are just detours.

Vincent van Gogh didn't start out as a painter—he tried being a teacher, a bookseller, even a preacher before he ever picked up a brush.

Harland Sanders (the guy who created KFC) was rejected **over a thousand times** before a restaurant finally agreed to use his chicken recipe.

Albert Einstein spent years being ignored by the academic world before anyone realized he was redefining physics.

Every single one of them **made decisions that "failed" before they succeeded.**

That's why the **worst decision isn't choosing wrong—it's choosing nothing at all.**

The Ghost Town Challenge: One Last Test

Right now, pick one decision you've been overthinking.

Now, close your eyes and imagine **you're the only person left on Earth.** No one is watching. No one will ever judge you. No one will ever know what you choose.

Now, what do you do?

That's your real answer.

So go do that.

CHAPTER VII

THE 'NO-PLAN' PLAN THAT CHANGES EVERYTHING

Most people believe success is about **having a plan.** A clear, structured, five-year roadmap that lays out exactly what you're going to do, how you're going to do it, and when you're going to achieve it.

You know who **didn't** have a plan?

- **Richard Branson, who started Virgin Airlines without a single business strategy**
- **Rick Rubin, who became one of the greatest music producers by telling artists to "do nothing"**
- **Mark Manson, who built a global empire by writing about why most self-help advice is useless**

They didn't succeed because they meticulously mapped out every step. They succeeded because they **took action before they were ready,** trusted momentum over structure, and let **the process shape the plan, not the other way around.**

If you've ever felt stuck because you don't know what the perfect first step is, **this chapter is for you.**

Richard Branson and the Airline That Wasn't Supposed to Exist

Richard Branson didn't wake up one day and think, You know what? I should start an airline.

He was stranded at an airport. That's it.

One day, in the 1980s, Branson was trying to fly from Puerto Rico to the British Virgin Islands when his flight got canceled. Instead of waiting around, he **chartered a private plane, borrowed a small blackboard, and wrote: "$39 one-way to the Virgin Islands"**. Then he walked around the airport, selling seats to the other stranded passengers.

That wasn't a business plan. That was **problem-solving in real-time**.

Virgin Airlines exists today because Branson didn't waste time **overthinking, making spreadsheets, or asking for permission**. He acted, then figured things out afterward.

Compare that to most people who sit on ideas for years, waiting for the **perfect moment** to execute. That moment never comes. Because the **best plans aren't made in a vacuum—they're made in motion**.

Why Rick Rubin's Greatest Advice is 'Do Nothing'

Rick Rubin, the legendary music producer behind some of the biggest albums of all time—Jay-Z, Adele, Red Hot Chili Peppers, Johnny Cash—has a bizarre creative philosophy.

When an artist is struggling in the studio, feeling uninspired, stuck in their own head, Rubin doesn't push them to work harder. He doesn't give them a structured plan.

Instead, he tells them: **"Do nothing."**

He believes that the worst thing you can do when you're trying to create something meaningful is to force it. Creativity doesn't work like an assembly line. It happens when you create space for **ideas to show up naturally.**

One of his most famous examples? Johnny Cash's album American IV: The Man Comes Around. By the time Rubin worked with Cash, the legendary singer's career was in decline. He was in poor health, struggling creatively, and unsure if he had anything left to give.

Instead of forcing a structured plan on Cash, Rubin just **let him sit in silence, explore old songs, and play whatever felt right.** The result? Cash's hauntingly raw cover of Hurt, a song that **became one of the most powerful musical moments of his career.**

Rubin's entire philosophy is built on the idea that **you don't need a rigid plan—sometimes, you just need to create the right conditions and let things happen.**

Mark Manson's 'Do Something' Principle: Why Winging It Works

Mark Manson became famous for writing The Subtle Art of Not Giving a F***, a book that flipped traditional self-help advice upside down.

One of his most important ideas? **The "Do Something" Principle.**

Manson argues that **most people don't take action because they're waiting for motivation,** waiting to feel ready, waiting for the perfect plan, waiting for everything to make sense.

But here's the twist: **Action creates motivation, not the other way around.**

He tells the story of how he built his writing career. He didn't have a master plan. He didn't have a publisher lined up. He didn't have a structured content calendar. He just started **writing one blog post at a time,** figuring things out as he went.

Now, millions of books later, people ask him, What was your plan?

The truth? **There was no plan.** There was just **doing something, and then adjusting along the way.**

Why 'Planning' is an Excuse for Not Starting

Most people over-plan because **planning feels productive.** You can sit around making lists, doing research, creating flowcharts, **convincing yourself you're working on something—when in reality, you're just avoiding the work itself.**

- You don't need to read 10 books about starting a business. You need to sell something.
- You don't need to take another course on writing. You need to start publishing.
- You don't need to map out every step before going to the gym. You need to do **one push-up right now.**

Planning is often just **procrastination dressed up in a fancy suit.**

And sure, there are times when strategy is important. But **strategy without execution is just a wish list.**

The No-Plan Plan in Action

So how do you apply this? Simple. **Instead of planning, set a ridiculously small action.**

1. Want to start a podcast? Record **one voice memo** on your phone today.

2. Want to launch a business? Sell **one thing** to **one person** right now.
3. Want to get fit? Drop to the floor and do **one push-up** this second.

You don't need **more clarity**. You need **momentum**.
Because the **best plans don't happen before action.**
They happen because of it.

How to Trick Your Brain into Taking Action Instantly

Your brain loves the illusion of safety. It loves over-planning because it feels **safe**, you're "working" without the risk of failure.

But your brain also responds to **urgency**. So if you want to break the cycle of overthinking, use this trick:
The Five-Minute Rule.

1. Pick something you've been delaying.
2. Set a timer for **five minutes**.
3. Work on it for those five minutes, no expectations, no pressure to be perfect. Just **start**.

What happens? **Momentum kicks in.** And once you start, it's **easier to keep going than it is to stop.**
This is why some of the most successful people in the world swear by **starting before they feel ready.**

- Jeff Bezos didn't wait until Amazon was perfect—he started selling books out of his garage.
- Picasso didn't wait for the "perfect" painting—he created over **50,000 works of art.**

- The Wright brothers didn't overthink—they just **built the damn airplane.**

None of them had a master plan. **They just took action, over and over again.**

Your Turn: The No-Plan Challenge

1. Pick something you've been putting off.
2. Start immediately, **no perfect plan, no second-guessing**.
3. Figure it out **as you go**.

The biggest lie we tell ourselves is that we need **a plan before we can begin.** But the truth is, **most of the time, you only figure out the plan by starting first.**

So stop waiting. **Start winging it.** Your future self will thank you.

Let's go deeper.

People love the illusion of control. It makes us feel safe, like we're steering our lives with precision, avoiding potholes, and accelerating toward success. That's why the idea of **not having a plan** terrifies most people.

But let's be honest, how many times in your life have things **actually** gone according to plan?

Think about it.

You probably didn't end up in the career you once thought you would. You didn't predict half the people who became your closest friends. You didn't anticipate the opportunities that shaped you or the setbacks that forced you to grow.

Life has already been throwing curveballs, and guess what? You **adjusted**. You figured things out.

So if winging it is already how you survive, why not **do it with intention?**

Why Structure Kills More Dreams Than It Creates

Schools, corporate jobs, and traditional goal-setting love structure. They teach you to create **linear** paths—Step A, leads to Step B, leads to Step C. It's neat. It's logical. It's comforting.

But real success? It happens in **zigzags**.

A study at Harvard found that **most entrepreneurs who built billion-dollar companies didn't start out with a perfect business plan.** Many of them pivoted multiple times, launching, failing, tweaking, adjusting—before they found what actually worked.

Sara Blakely, the billionaire founder of Spanx, didn't have a roadmap when she started. She had **one idea, $5,000 in savings, and zero experience in fashion.** When she tried to get manufacturers on board, **they all rejected her.** They didn't think a footless pantyhose idea would work.

A "logical" person would've stopped. She didn't.

Instead, she **kept adjusting, kept knocking on doors, kept winging it.** Eventually, she convinced a factory to produce her product, and today, she's one of the most successful self-made women in the world.

Imagine if she had waited to "figure it all out" before starting.

Waiting for a plan is just **procrastination with a fancier name.**

Why the Most Interesting People Are the Ones Who Say 'Yes' First

There are two types of people in this world:

1. The ones who need **certainty before they act**
2. The ones who **act before they're certain**

The first group waits for **guarantees, perfect conditions, and foolproof strategies**. They'll research for months, analyze every angle, and obsess over what-ifs—only to end up **never doing anything** because the plan is never "good enough."

The second group? They jump. They **figure things out in real-time**. They understand that **the best way to prepare is to start.**

This is how **Richard Branson** has launched over 400 companies. He doesn't sit around waiting to be "sure" of something. He just **says yes, then figures it out.**

It's why the **best travelers don't over-plan their trips.** They pick a place, pack a bag, and trust that adventure will unfold naturally.

It's why some of the most fascinating conversations happen when people go off-script instead of rigidly sticking to talking points.

People who act before they're ready? **They live stories worth telling.**

The Illusion of Readiness (and Why You'll Never Feel It)

Here's a lie we all believe at some point:

"I'll start when I'm ready."
Guess what? **You'll never feel ready.**
Neuroscience proves this.
Your brain is wired to **prioritize survival over progress.** It sees the unknown as a **threat,** even when that "threat" is just an uncomfortable conversation, a new project, or a big life change.

That's why people stay in mediocre jobs, relationships, and habits, they **feel safer than the unknown.**

But the second you **start** something? The fear shrinks.

A study at Columbia University found that **people who take action first experience a spike in confidence afterward,** not before. The action **creates** the confidence, not the other way around.

Think about a time you avoided something because you didn't feel ready, maybe public speaking, starting a fitness journey, or making a big decision.

Then think about when you finally did it.

You survived, didn't you?

Maybe you weren't perfect, but **you adapted in real-time.** And after it was over, you probably thought, Why did I wait so long?

That's the point.

The 'No-Plan' Test: What Would You Do If You Had to Start Today?

Let's try something.

Imagine that whatever you've been postponing, whether it's launching a project, switching careers, or learning a skill, **you HAVE to start today.**

Not next month. Not "when things calm down."

Today.

How would you begin?

Would you overanalyze? Or would you **figure out the smallest possible action and take it immediately?**

Maybe that's writing a terrible first draft.

Maybe that's sending an email you've been avoiding.

Maybe that's saying yes before you feel qualified.

Whatever it is, **it's better than waiting.**

Because waiting never makes you braver. **Starting does.**

The 'Fail Faster' Secret That Nobody Talks About

Here's something weird about successful people:

They actually **fail more than the average person.**

Not because they're reckless. But because **they take more shots.**

James Dyson, the guy who invented the Dyson vacuum? **5,126 failed prototypes.**

Oprah? **Fired from her first TV job.**

Vincent van Gogh? **Only sold one painting in his lifetime.**

The difference? **They didn't wait for the "right" time.** They started, messed up, learned, and **failed their way to success.**

And that's the real **No-Plan Plan**—to move before you have everything figured out, because figuring it out is part of the process.

What Happens When You Stop Waiting?

Something weird happens when you start **acting before you feel ready**—life starts moving **faster.**

Opportunities show up because you're putting yourself out there.

You meet people you never would've met while sitting in planning mode.

Your brain starts **adapting**, learning in real time, and actually **figuring things out** instead of just thinking about it.

The longer you wait, the more your brain builds up excuses.

The faster you act, the more **momentum** you create.

And momentum? That's what actually changes lives.

Your No-Plan Challenge: Do It Now

1. **Pick something you've been overthinking.** A decision. A project. A risk.
2. **Do ONE action today**—not tomorrow, not after research, not after a pep talk. **Today.**
3. **See what happens.** Because action leads to clarity, not the other way around.

Here's the truth—**every single successful person you admire started before they were ready.**

They didn't wait for confidence. They didn't wait for certainty.

They started, and **the plan figured itself out along the way.**

So what the hell are you waiting for?

CHAPTER VIII

YOUR LIFE IS A CASINO

I once knew a guy named Neil who spent five years trying to be the smartest person in every room. He'd read every productivity book, listened to hundreds of podcasts on 2x speed, and optimized every minute of his waking hours. I mean, the guy tracked his hydration level on an Excel sheet. **An Excel sheet for water**—talk about commitment.

And after all that, guess what happened?

Nothing. Absolutely nothing changed. Neil became a slightly healthier, slightly more hydrated, but infinitely more miserable person. Why? Because his life was so hyper-optimized that he'd accidentally stripped out the one thing his brain actually craved: **unexpected joy**.

Which brings us to something nobody ever tells you when you're chasing dopamine hits: **Your brain thrives on unpredictability, not predictability**. Yeah, routine is good. Habits are great. But if you want a brain that lights up like Times Square on New Year's Eve, you need to stop being so damn predictable.

That's why this chapter is called "**BREAK YOUR SCRIPT**".

It's not about quitting your job to backpack across Peru or tattooing inspirational quotes on your arm. It's about waking up tomorrow and doing something so random, so delightfully off-script that your brain goes, "Wait... what? I love this!"

And don't worry, I'm not sending you off to an ashram or forcing you to take cold showers at 5 AM. Let's get practical.

You ever wonder why some people can gamble in Vegas all night without getting tired? It's not because they're all irresponsible adults making questionable decisions (well, not only that). It's because casinos have figured out the ultimate dopamine hack: **random rewards.**

Scientists call this phenomenon "variable reward schedule," and casinos use it to keep you pulling levers and spinning wheels for hours. Basically, every now and then, you win a little—just enough to get excited, just unpredictable enough to keep you hooked. It's literally the reason you check your phone notifications every two minutes or refresh Instagram like your life depends on it.

Your brain loves surprises, unpredictability, and the thrill of not knowing exactly what comes next. And guess what? You can hack that principle and **turn your everyday life into a dopamine casino.** (Minus the shady floor carpets and free booze, unfortunately.)

Here's a story.

Let's meet Hannah. On paper, Hannah had her life figured out. Decent job, decent salary, decent relationship. She was the textbook definition of **fine.** You know the type. But deep down, she felt like her life was set to permanent beige. Safe, predictable, and let's face it, pretty dull.

Then one day, she decided to play a game with herself. She called it **"Flip The Coin."** Whenever she caught herself hesitating on something small, a coffee order, an evening walk, talking to a stranger at the café—she flipped a coin. Heads, she stuck to the usual; tails, she did the exact opposite.

The first time, she ended up ordering a cappuccino instead of her boring usual latte. Small win, but her brain felt a tiny buzz of excitement. Then the next day, she flipped a coin again and decided to walk home instead of taking the bus. And just like that, she found a street musician playing old-school jazz. She stood there, listening, smiling like an idiot for ten whole minutes.

One tiny act of randomness turned into another. Within a month, her life felt different. Nothing huge changed, but everything felt better.

She didn't quit her job. She didn't move cities. She just broke the script a little bit each day, and suddenly her brain felt like it was back online—fully charged, alive, noticing things again.

Let's talk neuroscience. The human brain releases dopamine whenever it encounters something new, interesting, or rewarding. It's basically nature's way of rewarding you for paying attention. And when you **always know what to expect**, your brain gets bored. It stops rewarding you. That's why you feel stuck, tired, and disconnected.

But small, random shifts, tiny acts of **deliberate unpredictability,** are like throwing little mental fireworks into your day. They jolt your brain awake, release bursts of dopamine, and remind you that life is full of possibilities.

Ever hear of the writer Hunter S. Thompson? Before writing each day, he'd pick a random book from his shelf, flip it open to a random page, and read exactly two sentences. Whatever he found, no matter how ridiculous, he'd use as inspiration for his first thought. It was like forcing his brain onto a creative rollercoaster.

And it works. It's why artists, entrepreneurs, and adventurers seem permanently energized—they don't live life like it's a boring grocery list. They treat life like a scavenger hunt, always leaving room for something spontaneous to happen.

Want your own dopamine-boosting mini-game? I've got you.

Tomorrow, before you start your day, set aside exactly ten minutes to play **The Serendipity Game.** Here's how:

Pick a random word—let's say "lemon." Now, your goal today is to somehow incorporate that word into a conversation naturally. Sounds easy, right? But it forces your brain to stay alert, pay attention, and look for an opening. Your brain stays on high-alert mode all day.

Or try **The Curiosity Challenge:**

At lunch, ask your friend or coworker the weirdest, most unconventional question you can think of. Don't be rude or invasive—just genuinely curious. "What's your biggest regret this week?" "When did you last embarrass yourself publicly?" The point isn't to be awkward—it's to stop having predictable, boring conversations.

Why does this matter? Because novelty doesn't just keep you entertained—it literally makes your brain smarter. Neuroscientist Dr. Moran Cerf says, "Our brains rewire fastest when exposed to novel experiences." Every unpredictable interaction, every strange encounter, every time you slightly step off your comfort track—your brain literally builds new neural connections.

And these new connections? They boost creativity, increase motivation, and flood your brain with dopamine. Suddenly, you're not just drifting through life—you're actively **shaping it into something more exciting.**

I know what you might be thinking—okay, sure, talking about lemons and flipping coins sounds nice, but will this really change my life? Let me ask you something: When was the last time you genuinely surprised yourself? When was the last time your day felt like a mini-adventure instead of a mini Groundhog Day?

Because most people, especially adults, stop surprising themselves. They fall into routines that are so structured they don't even realize how predictable their lives have become until they suddenly look around and wonder why nothing feels exciting anymore.

But here's the good news—you're not most people. If you've read this far, you're already wired differently. You're already tired of beige, predictable days. You're already searching for something more.

And all you have to do right now is **break your script**. Do one unexpected, random thing today. Then do another tomorrow. Your brain is begging you to stop doing the same thing every single day.

Because guess what? The most memorable days of your life probably weren't planned. They were spontaneous. The job opportunity you randomly said yes to. The friend you made when your flight got delayed. The love story that started with a chance encounter at a café. Life's best moments always come from **unscripted moments of randomness.**

So stop treating unpredictability like something you need to fix. It's not a bug—it's the whole damn feature. The future you want isn't waiting at the end of a perfectly planned path. It's waiting on the other side of a choice you never thought you'd make, a risk you never saw coming, an adventure you accidentally said yes to.

All you have to do is be brave enough to break your routine and say, "Okay, universe, surprise me."

And trust me—once you taste the thrill of living with just a little unpredictability, you'll never go back to beige again.

Ready to break your script? Good.

Life's about to get interesting.

Alright, let's get serious, but in a fun way, because nobody likes a boring lecture about "embracing change." You already know life is more exciting when you mix things up. But let's make this **real**.

I'm not here to give you vague motivational nonsense like "Just go out there and do something different!" No. We're going full scientist-meets-mischief-maker mode.

You're about to **hack your brain** into loving unpredictability so much that it actively starts craving excitement instead of numbing itself with doom scrolling and whatever TV show Netflix keeps shoving at you.

First, let's introduce you to **your own brain's biggest glitch**.

Your Brain is a Lazy Genius (And That's a Problem)

See, your brain is an efficiency machine. It's obsessed with **predictability** because it saves energy. This is why your morning routine feels automatic, why you can drive home without remembering the trip, and why you wear the same three outfits even though your closet is full.

Predictability = Less thinking = More energy saved.

Sounds great, right? Wrong. Because while this system is useful for survival, it's absolutely **terrible for happiness**.

When everything in your life becomes predictable, your brain **stops rewarding you with dopamine.**

This is why time feels slower when you're a kid, everything is new. You're constantly learning, messing up, laughing at dumb things, getting surprised. But as an adult? You've been there, done that. Your days start blending together, and suddenly you're wondering why your life feels like it's on autoplay.

Here's the truth: If you don't **manually** inject unpredictability into your life, your brain won't do it for you.

That's why we're about to trick your brain into **falling in love with randomness again.**

The 'Dopamine Bomb' Exercises (Try at Your Own Risk)

Let's make things fun. You don't need to go skydiving or move to a new country to feel alive again. You just need **small, controlled doses of unpredictability** every day.

1. The Yes Day Experiment

For **one full day**, you have to say **YES** to everything that doesn't endanger your life or land you in jail.

- Coworker invites you for lunch at a weird new place? Yes.
- Friend wants to try a dance class even though you have two left feet? Yes.
- Barista asks if you want to try their secret menu drink? Yes.

The whole point? You **don't** overthink. You **don't** plan. You **just say yes** and see what happens.

99% of the time, nothing bad happens. In fact, you'll probably have more fun in **one day** than you've had in weeks.

2. The Random Route Game

Instead of taking your usual path home, open Google Maps, spin around, and drop a pin **somewhere random** within 5 miles. That's your new route home today.

This does two things:

1. **Forces your brain to wake up.** New scenery = More dopamine.
2. **Increases your chances of a random adventure.** Maybe you find a hidden café. Maybe you stumble upon a street musician. Maybe nothing happens except you realize how much you usually operate on autopilot.

Either way, **your brain will thank you for the surprise.**

3. The 'Do The Opposite' Challenge

Think of **one** small thing you do every day. Now do the opposite.

- Always sit in the same spot at your favorite café? **Pick a different table.**
- Always order the same coffee? **Choose something totally different.**
- Always listen to the same kind of music? **Find a random playlist in a new genre.**

Small? Yes. But **every time you break a pattern, your brain gets a tiny dopamine hit.**

4. The Compliment Ambush

Next time you're out, you have to compliment **three strangers.** Could be their outfit, their hair, their energy—whatever feels natural.

Why? Because **breaking social scripts is the ultimate dopamine hack.**

You'll see how small actions create **unexpected ripples,** maybe someone laughs, maybe you make their day, maybe they compliment you back. Either way, **your brain lights up because it wasn't expecting the interaction.**

Crossing things off this list will give you **more dopamine than achieving fake goals ever will.**

Why Doing 'Stupid' Things Is Actually Genius

You ever notice that kids **laugh 300 times a day** while adults barely hit 15?

It's not because life gets objectively less fun, it's because we stop **doing dumb things just for the hell of it.**

Here's a radical idea: **Do things just because.**

- Buy the most ridiculous hat in a store and wear it for a day.
- Make up a fake backstory when a stranger asks what you do.
- Host a **backwards dinner party** where everyone starts with dessert and ends with appetizers.

Why? Because breaking **pointless** rules is where dopamine **lives.**

What Happens When You Start Playing With Life Again

When you **break your routine on purpose**, something weird happens.

- Your mind starts paying attention again.
- You remember what it feels like to be **curious** instead of just getting through the day.
- You stop waiting for a "perfect" life to arrive and start making every day feel interesting **on purpose.**

Remember Hannah from earlier? The one who played the Flip The Coin game?

Two months into doing that, she ended up in a city she'd never been to, at a live music event she never would've gone to, talking to a person she never would've met—and that person ended up offering her an opportunity that changed her entire career.

All because of **one random decision.**

Now, will every flip of the coin lead to something life-changing? No. But **it will make your brain love waking up again.**And that's worth more than any perfectly structured routine.

Your Life Is Already a Casino—Play the Damn Game

Here's what you need to remember:

- Your brain is a dopamine machine that craves **surprises, novelty, and fun.**
- Small, random changes trick your brain into **feeling alive again.**
- The most interesting people aren't the ones with perfect plans—they're the ones who **let curiosity lead.**

So here's your final challenge:

Do **one weird, unexpected thing today.** Something that **slightly** breaks your script.

And if you feel that tiny **buzz** of excitement? That's your brain **waking up** again.

You don't need to travel the world or overhaul your life. You just need to **start playing with it.**

Your dopamine jackpot is waiting.

Now go spin the wheel.

CHAPTER IX

THE 'MONK & THE ROCKSTAR'

There are two kinds of people in the world:

1. The **Monks**—obsessed with discipline, structure, clean eating, 5 AM workouts, and deleting social media like it's radioactive waste.
2. The **Rockstars**—chasing highs, living fast, indulging in every pleasure, burning out, and then somehow rising from the ashes like a chaotic phoenix.

Now, let's be real: **Neither one of these extremes is sustainable.**

If you're too much of a monk, life becomes a never-ending **self-improvement project**, a hamster wheel of optimization that sucks the joy out of living.

If you're too much of a rockstar, life turns into a **dopamine crash-and-burn cycle,** a series of quick hits that leave you empty, exhausted, and wondering why the hell everything feels meaningless.

So what's the solution? **You need both.**

You need to know **when to be a monk** and **when to be a rockstar**—when to go all-in on discipline and when to say screw it, let's have some fun.

Welcome to the **Monk & Rockstar Balance Formula,** the art of **cycling between calm dopamine and high dopamine so you get the best of both worlds without wrecking yourself.**

Naval's 'Calm Dopamine' Rule: How to Get High Without the Crash

Naval Ravikant, the philosopher-investor who somehow always sounds like a modern-day Buddha with Wi-Fi, has a concept called **"calm dopamine."**

Here's the idea: Most of the dopamine hits we chase, social media, junk food, binging Netflix, impulsive shopping, are **fast, easy, and instantly rewarding**. But they come with a cost. The more we indulge, the **harder it becomes to feel happy without them.**

That's why Naval is obsessed with **slower, long-lasting dopamine sources:**

- **Reading books instead of scrolling Twitter.**
- **Going for a walk instead of taking another coffee shot.**
- **Lifting weights instead of chasing an adrenaline high.**

He says, "A fit body, a calm mind, and a house full of love. These things cannot be bought. They must be earned."

In other words: **Real happiness comes from playing the long game.**

So, does this mean you should **never** indulge in short-term dopamine? No. That's where our next guy comes in.

Tim Ferriss' 'Mini-Retirement' Trick: Why You Should Party Like a Rockstar (Strategically)

Tim Ferriss, the author of The 4-Hour Workweek, isn't just about optimizing productivity—he's also about **strategic** indulgence.

One of his biggest lessons? **You don't need to wait until you're 65 to enjoy life.**

Most people **grind relentlessly** for years, hoping they'll finally get to enjoy life later. But Ferriss flips the script, he **intentionally takes long breaks (mini-retirements) between intense work cycles.**

He'll go **hard for months**, writing, working, and building businesses. Then, he'll completely **disappear to surf in Argentina, learn a new skill, or just do nothing for a while.**

This is the **Rockstar Phase—intense pleasure, full immersion, zero guilt.**

Then, when it's time to get back to work, he **switches to Monk Mode,** clean routines, discipline, and focused deep work.

Ferriss' whole philosophy is about **balancing structured discipline with bursts of indulgence.**

What does this mean for you?

It means **you can enjoy your guilty pleasures guilt-free,** as long as you're **intentional about them.**

The Dalai Lama's Surprisingly Chill Views on Pleasure

If anyone should be fully team Monk, it's the Dalai Lama, right?

Wrong.

When someone once asked him if monks should drink alcohol, he didn't say, Absolutely not! He simply shrugged and said, "Moderation is key."

He also openly enjoys cookies. That's right—the spiritual leader of millions has a **sweet tooth.**

Why does this matter? Because **even the most disciplined people in the world don't believe in total restriction.**

A completely dopamine-free life **isn't enlightened—it's just boring.**

The Dalai Lama understands something most productivity gurus don't: **Happiness isn't about constant discipline. It's about knowing when to relax and enjoy yourself.**

The Monk & Rockstar Balance Formula (How to Apply It in Real Life)

You don't need to pick one path forever. You just need to **switch modes intentionally.**

1. Set 'Monk Mode' and 'Rockstar Mode' Timeframes
Instead of chasing balance daily (which is exhausting), **split your life into cycles.**

For example:

- **Monk Mode (4 weeks)** → Wake up early, eat clean, work deeply, avoid distractions.
- **Rockstar Mode (1 week)** → Stay out late, try new experiences, indulge in the things you love.

This keeps you from **burning out on discipline** while avoiding the **crash of overindulgence.**

2. Flip the 'Pleasure Guilt' Mindset
Most people indulge in guilty pleasures, then immediately beat themselves up for it. **That's dumb.**

Instead, **plan your indulgence** so that when you're in Rockstar Mode, you can **enjoy it fully without guilt.**

For example:

- Love video games? **Schedule a full Rockstar weekend of gaming.**
- Want a lazy movie night? **Own it—no guilt, no productivity pressure.**
- Craving a wild night out? **Go all in, but know when to switch back.**

This way, you **squeeze the most joy out of pleasure** instead of ruining it with guilt.

3. Use 'Anchor Rituals' to Switch Between Modes

Your brain needs **clear signals** when shifting between Monk and Rockstar phases.

Try these rituals:

- **Ending Rockstar Mode?** Do a 24-hour detox—drink tons of water, sleep early, journal, and reset.
- **Entering Monk Mode?** Do something symbolic—clean your workspace, meditate, or start a fresh notebook.
- **Exiting Monk Mode?** Celebrate with a deliberate indulgence—one amazing meal, one fun event, something that feels like a reward.

These rituals **help your brain transition smoothly** without the usual guilt or burnout.

4. Stop Living in the 'Grey Zone'

Most people fail at balance because they **never fully commit to either side.**

They don't go full Monk Mode (because discipline is hard).

They don't go full Rockstar Mode (because guilt creeps in).

So they end up in **a half-assed in-between state**—always working but never focused, always relaxing but never fully enjoying it.

Solution? **Go all in.**

- If you're in Monk Mode, **lock in.** No distractions, no indulgence, full focus.
- If you're in Rockstar Mode, **let go.** No guilt, no stress, full experience.

Half-committing to both just makes you feel like you're failing at both.

Your Brain is Happiest When It Has Contrast

Ever noticed how **hot coffee tastes better on a cold day?**
How **music sounds better after silence?**
How **food is ten times more satisfying when you're starving?**

That's because **contrast creates pleasure.**

Monk Mode makes Rockstar Mode **more exciting.**
Rockstar Mode makes Monk Mode **more productive.**

You don't need a **perfect** balance. You just need to **intentionally switch modes when it's time.**

So next time you feel guilty for indulging or frustrated with discipline, remember—**you're not supposed to be just a Monk or just a Rockstar.**

You're both.

Now go play the game right.

Let me tell you about a guy named Arjun.

Arjun was stuck in the **grey zone**—the place where most people spend their lives. Not fully committed to his work, but not fully enjoying his downtime either. He'd spend hours watching productivity videos but never actually execute anything. He'd go out with friends but keep checking his emails, convincing himself he was "being responsible."

He wasn't a Monk. He wasn't a Rockstar. He was just... tired.

One day, his friend challenged him: **"What if you did everything at 100%? Full focus when you work, full indulgence when you play?"**

Arjun was skeptical, but he decided to try.

For **two weeks, he went into full Monk Mode.**

- Woke up at 6 AM.
- No social media.
- Deep work blocks with zero distractions.
- Gym every evening.
- Meditated daily.

At first, it was uncomfortable. His brain craved mindless scrolling, junk food, lazy distractions. But after a few days? **Something shifted.**

His energy skyrocketed. He finished projects in half the time. He felt **clear-headed, sharper, unstoppable.**

Then, after two weeks, he switched.

For **one week, he went full Rockstar Mode.**

- Late nights with friends.
- Ate what he wanted, guilt-free.
- No alarms, no rigid schedules.
- Travel, fun, spontaneity.

And guess what? He **enjoyed it 10x more than before,** because for the first time, he wasn't half-working while relaxing. He wasn't carrying guilt. He was **fully in the moment.**

By the end of the month, his entire mindset had shifted. He wasn't trying to find balance—**balance was happening naturally.**

That's when he realized:

Balance isn't about doing everything at once.

It's about doing **one thing fully, then the other fully.**

How This One Shift Can Change Everything for You

Most people feel exhausted not because they're overworked, but because they're **half-working and half-relaxing all the time.**

- **At work?** They're distracted.
- **At home?** They're still thinking about work.
- **On vacation?** They check emails "just in case."
- **Trying to relax?** They feel guilty for not being productive.

This is why you always feel like you're **never doing enough—but also never truly enjoying yourself.**

That ends today.

Because once you **commit fully to each phase,** work when you work, play when you play, you'll unlock something magical: **total energy recovery.**

You won't need "balance" every single day because **your life will naturally balance itself over time.**

How to Build Your Monk & Rockstar Lifestyle (Without Overhauling Your Life)

If you want to start using this formula, you don't need to change everything at once.

Step 1: Pick Your Cycle Length

You can switch between Monk Mode and Rockstar Mode **in cycles that fit your life:**

- **Daily Balance:** Work hard during the day, fully relax at night.
- **Weekly Balance:** 5 days of deep focus, 2 days of indulgence.
- **Monthly Balance:** 2-3 weeks of intense structure, 1 week of full enjoyment.

Don't overthink it—just pick a rhythm and start.

Step 2: Define Your Monk Mode Rules

When you're in Monk Mode, you need clear rules. No half-measures.

Example Monk Mode rules:

- Wake up and sleep at the same time every day.
- Set work goals and eliminate all distractions.
- Exercise and eat clean.
- No unnecessary social media or mindless consumption.
- Meditate or reflect daily.

The key here? **Monk Mode should feel like an intentional push toward your highest self.**

Step 3: Define Your Rockstar Mode Rules

Rockstar Mode isn't just "doing whatever you want." It's **structured indulgence.**

Example Rockstar Mode rules:

- Sleep in if you want to.
- Eat the food you love—without guilt.
- Say yes to spontaneous plans.
- Take risks, try new things, enjoy the moment.
- Don't obsess over productivity—let things unfold naturally.

The key here? **Rockstar Mode should feel like a reward, not a relapse.**

Step 4: Build Transition Rituals

Your brain needs a **clear signal** when you're switching between modes.

- **Ending Rockstar Mode?** Do a reset—hydrate, stretch, journal, clean your space.
- **Entering Monk Mode?** Set up your environment—remove distractions, set goals, establish routines.
- **Exiting Monk Mode?** Celebrate—do something fun, go out, enjoy yourself guilt-free.

Without these **rituals**, your brain will resist the switch. But once you create **intentional transitions**, shifting between modes becomes effortless.

Why This Works (Even If You Think It Won't)

This system isn't just theory. It's how some of the world's most successful people operate.

Elon Musk? Monk Mode for work, Rockstar Mode for wild parties.

Warren Buffett? Deep focus on investing, full indulgence in playing the ukulele and junk food.

Anthony Bourdain? Intense, focused chef life, then full Rockstar travel and indulgence.

Even the most disciplined athletes—like Cristiano Ronaldo or Serena Williams—**have cycles of extreme training followed by complete recovery.**

Because the body and brain **thrive on contrast.**

If you always stay in Monk Mode, you'll burn out. If you always stay in Rockstar Mode, you'll self-destruct. But if you **intentionally cycle between them?** You unlock a life that's both **productive and fulfilling.**

Your Challenge: Build Your First Monk & Rockstar Cycle

You're not going to just read this and move on. You're going to **apply it**—today.

Here's your challenge:

1. **Pick your next cycle.** Will you do Monk Mode for a week? Two weeks? Pick a timeframe.
2. **Set clear rules.** Write them down—what will Monk Mode look like for you? What about Rockstar Mode?
3. **Decide when you'll switch.** Schedule your next Rockstar Mode phase **so you don't burn out.**
4. **Commit 100%.** No half-effort. When you're in Monk Mode, be **all in.** When you're in Rockstar Mode, enjoy it **without guilt.**

What Happens When You Get This Right?

Something crazy happens when you stop living in the grey zone.

- **Your work gets 10x better.** You're not half-distracted anymore. Deep focus becomes your new normal.
- **Your fun gets 10x better.** You stop checking your phone at dinner. You actually **enjoy the moment.**
- **You stop feeling exhausted.** Because you're not always in limbo, you're either fully ON or fully OFF.

And the best part? **You start to love both sides.**

You'll crave Monk Mode because it makes you powerful.

You'll crave Rockstar Mode because it makes life worth living.

Suddenly, everything clicks.

You stop wondering how to "balance work and life." Because now, your life **balances itself.**

And that? That's when you know you're doing it right.

Welcome to the Monk & Rockstar Life.

Now go live it.

CHAPTER X

REWRITE YOUR CODE

Let's get one thing straight: **you were never broken.**

If you've ever felt lost, stuck, or like you're just drifting through life, it's not because something is wrong with you. It's because nobody ever handed you the damn **source code** to how life actually works.

You were thrown into this world with outdated instructions:

- Work hard, be responsible, follow the rules.
- Chase success, chase stability, chase whatever society tells you to want.
- Be productive every second, optimize your life, and never waste time.

And then, when that formula didn't make you happy, you were told, Maybe you're just not trying hard enough.

That's a lie.

The real problem? **You've been running on old software.**

Your mind is like an operating system, full of scripts you never questioned. And those scripts—your habits, your beliefs, your automatic thoughts, **are controlling your life.**

But here's the kicker: **You can rewrite them.**

And that's what we're doing right now.

No more default settings. No more outdated scripts. No more playing the game on someone else's terms.

It's time to **update your system, delete the garbage code, and install the mindset that actually lets you live.**

Why Most People Never Change (And How You Will)

There are two kinds of people in the world:

1. **The Default People**—those who accept whatever life throws at them, running on autopilot, too distracted to even realize they have a choice.
2. **The Hackers**—those who break the system, rewrite the code, and build the life they actually want.

Most people? **Default mode.**

They complain about their job but don't leave.
They want to be healthier but never change their habits.
They hate their routine but repeat it every single day.

Why? Because **changing your code requires effort,** and most people are too busy scrolling to even consider it.

But here's where you're different.

You made it to this chapter. You're here, right now, because **somewhere deep inside, you already know you're capable of rewriting your own rules.**

So let's start.

Step One: Identify Your Broken Code

Think of your mind like an old-school computer. If you keep running the same glitchy software, your system will **always crash in the same places.**

Look at your patterns.

- Where do you always get stuck?
- What do you keep saying you'll change, but never do?
- What do you secretly know is holding you back?

Most people never stop to **audit their own programming,** they just assume that's how they are. But if your life keeps repeating itself, it's because you're **running the same script over and over.**

It's time to **debug.**

Step Two: Burn The Old Script

There's a reason burning things feels so satisfying—it's a **hard reset.**

So let's do something radical.

Write down every outdated belief you've been carrying.

Seriously. Open your notes app. Grab a piece of paper. Right now.

Write down everything you've told yourself that isn't serving you anymore.

- I'm not good enough to do XYZ.
- I can't change because this is just who I am.
- I'll start later, when I feel ready.

Now? **Delete it. Burn it. Shred it.**

This is your first real software update.

You are **not your old stories.** You are **not your past choices.**

You are whatever you choose to be **starting right now.**

Step Three: Install the New Operating System

If you want a different life, you need **new rules to run on.**
    Try these:

1. **If you don't like it, change it.** Immediately. No waiting for motivation. No waiting for the perfect moment.
2. **You're not stuck—you're just repeating a habit.** The moment you do one thing differently, you've already started changing.
3. **Nobody is coming to save you.** This isn't a bad thing. It's the best news you'll ever hear. **You have full control.**
4. **Confidence is a byproduct of action.** Stop waiting to "feel ready." Readiness is a lie. Move first, confidence follows.
5. **Your comfort zone is a prison disguised as safety.** Escape before it locks you in forever.
6. **If it's scary, it's probably worth doing.** The best things in life live on the other side of discomfort.

These aren't just motivational quotes—they're the **laws of rewiring your life.**
    Your brain will resist at first. It loves the old software. It loves patterns, even the bad ones.
    But every time you **act against the old script**, you're installing something new.

Step Four: Build The 'Proof of Change' Loop

Here's why most people fail at self-improvement:
    They **don't see immediate proof that they've changed,** so they give up and go back to their default settings.

You? **You're going to build a proof loop.**

1. **Do one tiny thing today that proves you've already started changing.** (Even if it's as small as drinking water before coffee.)
2. **Tomorrow, do it again, and add something else.**
3. **Every day, stack one more 'proof' that you are not your old code anymore.**

It can be as small as saying no to something that doesn't serve you.

As simple as walking for five minutes instead of scrolling TikTok.

As quick as standing up straighter when you feel like shrinking.

Change isn't about one huge moment—it's about **a million small proofs that you're already on a new path.**

Step Five: Make This Book Your Bible

Listen, life isn't a one-time transformation.

This isn't a Disney movie where you have an epiphany and everything is fixed forever. **You will relapse into old patterns.** You will get lazy. You will forget what you learned here.

That's why you need a **reset button.**

This book? This chapter? **It's your reset button.**

Whenever you feel stuck, lost, or slipping back into old patterns, **come back here.**

Read it again.

Reinstall the new code.

Remind yourself who the hell you are.

Because once you rewrite your script, **you never go back to living the default life again.**

You know too much now.

And the world? **The world better be ready for what you're about to do next.**

Now go. Break the code. Rewrite the story. And don't look back.

Let's talk about something nobody ever tells you: **reinvention isn't a one-time event.**

You don't just wake up one day, rewrite your life script, and suddenly transform into a brand-new, unstoppable version of yourself. That's a movie montage, not real life.

In reality? Reinvention is **messy**. It's full of false starts, failed attempts, and moments where you wonder if you're just kidding yourself.

You'll have days where you feel like a goddamn superhero, and then the next day, you'll catch yourself slipping back into old habits, scrolling, procrastinating, overthinking, doubting everything you just promised yourself.

And when that happens, you might start thinking, Maybe I haven't really changed. Maybe I'm just built this way.

No. That's the old code talking.

The truth is, **change isn't a straight line—it's a spiral.**

Every time you relapse, every time you fall back into an old pattern, **you're not back at square one.**

You're just being tested.

Think of it like leveling up in a game. When you're at Level 1, the enemies are weak. Easy. But as soon as you start upgrading, better weapons, better skills, the game doesn't get easier. **The enemies get harder.**

That's what happens when you start rewriting your life.

The moment you decide, I'm not playing by my old rules anymore, the universe doesn't just roll over and say, Great, here's your new, improved life on a silver platter!

Nope.

It throws tests at you.

You say you want discipline? Here's a late-night craving for distraction.

You say you want confidence? Here's an uncomfortable situation that forces you to prove it.

You say you want freedom? Here's a choice between the safe, predictable path and the scary, uncertain one.

It's like the universe wants to know: **Are you serious, or are you just talking?**

And most people? They take these setbacks as signs that change isn't possible for them. That maybe they were meant to stay the same.

But not you.

Because now? **You know the game.**

The game isn't about avoiding challenges. It's about **responding differently when they show up.**

Every time you break an old pattern, even in the smallest way, you're **winning.**

Every time you pause before reacting in your usual way, every time you catch yourself before falling into an old loop, every time you do something slightly different than before—you're **rewiring your brain.**

And rewiring takes time.

Think about a hiking trail that's been walked on a thousand times. The path is clear, easy to follow, and automatic. That's how your old habits work. Your brain **defaults to the path it knows best.**

Now imagine trying to create a **brand-new path** through a dense forest. The first time? It's rough. Messy.

You have to push through branches, clear the way, and it feels like you're getting nowhere.

But the more you walk it? The clearer it becomes.

Eventually? It **becomes the new automatic path.**

That's what you're doing when you rewrite your code. You're **building a new mental trail**, and every time you choose the new path, even just once, you're making it easier for Future You.

So don't expect change to be clean. Expect it to be **chaotic, weird, uncomfortable, and full of moments where you doubt yourself.**

But also? **Expect it to work.**

Because if you keep going, even when you mess up, even when it feels slow, even when it feels like nothing is happening, one day, you'll look back and realize:

Holy sht. I'm not the same person anymore.

And that? That moment? **That's everything.**

You don't need to be perfect.

You don't need to have it all figured out.

You just need to keep choosing the new path, one tiny decision at a time.

Because that's how you win.

And you?

You were always meant to win.

To The One Reading

Dear warrior,

I know you have been told that you're strong, you are a warrior— a survivor, but I know deep down you, just like me, need a shoulder to lean on. You have been strong for many years, your battles have been silent, your tears have dried, and your heart now aches.

I see you, I know you. I am you. I have been there right in your shoes and I promise you that if you have reached here, till this page— it gets better from here.

It's time to get up, rub off the dust on your knees, put a pretty bandaid on your wounds and become the main character of your story. It's time you decide to take control of your life and choose yourself.

Not because you've just finished a 'self-help' book or because I am telling you to. You need to choose yourself over everything now, this very moment, this very second because this life is short and we only have a handful of moments to make memories out of.

If you do not embrace yourself with love today and snatch the pen from the hands of destiny to write your own story, who will?

You've got this, my friend. After all, you are a warrior.
But also a saviour. Starting with yourself.

Yours truly
Just another girl who decided to save herself!

www.ingramcontent.com/pod-product-compliance
Lightning Source LLC
Chambersburg PA
CBHW020558160726
47991CB00002B/780